A Mother's Diary

A Mother's Diary

Personal Diary Entries Shared by Moms
to Help Their Daughters Navigate Life

KIANA SHAW

A MOTHER'S DIARY
Published by Purposely Created Publishing Group™
Copyright © 2018 Kiana Shaw

All rights reserved.

No part of this book may be reproduced, distributed or transmitted in any form by any means, graphic, electronic, or mechanical, including photocopy, recording, taping, or by any information storage or retrieval system, without permission in writing from the publisher, except in the case of reprints in the context of reviews, quotes, or references.

Unless otherwise indicated, scripture quotations are from the Holy Bible, King James Version. All rights reserved.

Scriptures marked NIV are taken from the New International Version®. Copyright © 1973, 1978, 1984, 2011 by Biblica, Inc.™. All rights reserved.

Printed in the United States of America
ISBN: 978-1-949134-23-0

Special discounts are available on bulk quantity purchases by book clubs, associations and special interest groups. For details email: sales@publishyourgift.com or call (888) 949-6228.

For information logon to:
www.PublishYourGift.com

Dedication

This book is dedicated to daughters, bonus daughters, nieces, little sisters, and granddaughters everywhere who feel they are going through unique situations that no one else would understand and who are struggling to find their way on their own. Also, to the young ladies who currently can't hear the voices of their own moms—even though they are doing their best to listen—because they are having a difficult time while trying to find their own voices.

This project has been a labor of love shared by a group of super-mommies; we have taken the time to search our own hearts, consciences, and pasts to share the very best of our experiences, and we hope that our knowledge and know-how will bless and aid you in making better decisions in this complicated journey called life. We are bearing it all and openly sharing with you our real-life experiences; these are true stories, and many of them reveal the pitfalls that we've encountered and how we (sometimes barely) recovered from them. We hope to encourage, inspire, and enrich the lives of every young woman that picks up this book—up to and including our very own daughters.

This book is also dedicated to all the mothers, bonus moms, aunts, big sisters, and grandmothers who have tried to impart wisdom to the young ladies in their lives, only to be misunderstood, accused of not being supportive, or shut out. We know you also have experiences to share and that you silently understand the cries of your daughters. Take heart; we are sharing our stories for you and with you in hopes that you too will know that you aren't alone in this journey called womanhood.

Enjoy, and strap on your seatbelt, because you are in for one heck of a ride!

Table of Contents

Foreword 1

Preface 3

A MOTHER'S DIARY

Anjanette Robinson
We're Not Always Ready for Sex 5

April Mack
Running from a Bully Nearly Cost Me Everything 13

Ashley Shaw
Sometimes Danger Lurks Instead of Fun 23

Dee French
Don't Forget to Breathe 33

Ereena George
Ugly Feet Made Me Dislike Myself 43

Ginca Love
God's Plan Is Still in Full Effect 53

Jennifer Smith
Three Strikes Doesn't Mean You're Out 63

Kiana Shaw
My First Love Was Not Lovely at All 75

Mara Monique
Being Grown Doesn't Come from Age 85

Tasha Champion
When You're Racing Yourself, You're Going to Lose 99

Tiffany Adams
My Brother Was My Personal Angel 109

Yolanda Allen
Sometimes You Have to Grow Through
What You Go Through 119

A DAUGHTER'S HANDBOOK

Anjanette Robinson
Dear Jefferionna 133

April Mack
Dear Leila and Parker 135

Ashley Shaw
Dear Lil' Ashley 137

Dee French
Dear Jana 141

Ereena George
Dear Jelani 144

Ginca Love
Dear Alana, Genise, and Kaaliyah 147

Jennifer Smith
Dear Jozalynn 150

Kiana Shaw
Dear Kayla 154

Mara Monique
Dear DeNarae and DaeLynn 159

Tasha Champion
Dear Destiny 162

Tiffany Adams
Dear Breanna and Teyanna 165

Yolanda Allen
My Dearest Daughters 168

Afterword 171

About the Authors 173

Foreword

Of course, I could start with the opening every mother would write: I love my daughter. I am proud of my daughter! I am *not* surprised at her achievements. (I mean, she is MY child.) I am in awe of her life. I have her back unconditionally.

But allow me to go into a little more depth: Kiana is always thinking ahead, always in charge, and always the first to voice her opinion! Even back in preschool (I said always), when the teacher had to leave the classroom Kiana was left in charge to monitor and hold the class accountable. She would read to the students (from memory—she is a bit of a perfectionist) and keep stern control of the class.

She is a woman who believes we all have choices and that all of our choices have consequences; while Kiana has made incorrect choices, she learned from their consequences and has emerged even more powerful! She uses this power to get up, step up, and move up to her next level of life.

The advice she gives here is not simply words quoted from a book; it is straight from her humbled heart that has endured and learned and now empowers others from her experiences. Reading this book will give you the same boldness to overcome your obstacles and challenges and will give you power in your own lives to make integrity-based decisions.

God's purpose for Kiana is to save young ladies; sometimes that means one today, two tomorrow, and three the next day instead of many at once. But she takes that to heart, and every day she gets up and walks in her purpose.

Pamela Jones
Proud mother, grandmother, sister, aunt, and friend

Preface

When I first thought of this project, it was two separate ideas. I wanted to create something that would help teenage girls everywhere to know and understand that their mothers—and the other women in their lives who provide guidance—are not instructing them out of a desire to make them little angels who do no wrong. Instead, I wanted them to understand that those women who chastise them, correct them, fuss at them, encourage them, etc., are really speaking from a place of experience—experience that hurt those women and brought them to their knees, some even to the point of suicide.

I really want young ladies who read this to understand that people have gone before them in this life, and that a lot of us have already experienced the things they will encounter. We already know how to avoid them. We already know how hurtful they are and we already know how to come out of them. I believe God allowed us to have some of these experiences just so we could turn around and help the young ladies in our lives avoid them—and so we could help the young ladies pull through when they don't heed the warnings.

I hope to help the teenage readers of this book understand: our harsh tones and sometimes hurtful words are truly coming from a place of fear. Fear that they won't make it out of a situation or that they will repeat their mistakes, as many of us did. Fear that, like us, they will carry the burden of the consequences of those actions.

I don't want them to have to struggle. Perhaps that is the biggest disconnect between mothers and daughters; we are trying to prevent them from having experiences that they *want* to have.

So I wanted to do a project that allows teenage girls to read our personal stories and understand that they alone have the power to change the trajectory of their lives. These stories are shared so that young ladies across the globe can learn from our experiences and make better choices than we did.

My second idea was to create a platform where mothers could write their daughters love letters. However, I find that young ladies need to trust us before they will believe us, and the best way to get them to trust us is to relate to them through our stories. It helps them authenticate us before they spend time listening to us. So this project is a merge of these thoughts, and it is my prayer that mothers and daughters alike will enjoy this book.

Kiana Shaw
Master Personal Development Coach

Anjanette Robinson

Dear Diary: We're Not Always Ready for Sex

One day when I was thirteen years old, I went to go spend the week with my dearest friend, Maxi, and some of my family who lived nearby. I had not seen any of them in quite some time and I was excited at just the thought of the fun we were going to have.

When I got there Maxi was eager to introduce me to her new friends. I prepared myself like a Barbie doll: hair whipped into a feather style, favorite jeans fitting just right, looking fly! They were excited too, getting to meet the fly girl from Compton who had it going on.

They pulled out all the stops to show me a good time. The entertainment of video games, music, and movies was non-stop. We hung out late every night because her parents felt her community was safe. As long as we didn't leave the apartment building, we could do as we pleased—which worked out pretty good for me once I caught the eye of one of the young men.

He was really nice to me in the beginning, buying me soda and chips, and he even gave me a keychain with his name on it. That really was all it took to make me feel special, but it was the added "celebrity" treatment of everyone wanting to know me and be my friend that had me feeling as though I was poppin'.

All that attention went to my head and I started being too cool. His sweet nothings and the speed at which I became the big fish in that small pond made me feel bigger than life, so I decided to go to the next level of my newfound freedom and have sex with him that week. I was feeling very grown-up, after all, so why not seal the deal? And sex was something you did to be cool, I thought. Well, the sex was all right, but it wasn't all I had expected it to be.

The next day, we all decided to go swimming—and reality caught up to me quickly. All those blonde-haired, blue-eyed kids got to see my nappy hair and ashy skin. No one had a pressing comb because, being white, they didn't have a need for one. Without a hot comb, my hair drew up into its natural, shorter state. So the group of kids that loved me a few hours before suddenly started to tease me. Talk about a fall from grace! I hoped that the young man I had shared myself with would still be nice, but apparently that was too much to ask for. He no longer wanted to claim me as his girlfriend because he was embarrassed of me. I really had thought they were my friends, but they teased me, called me names, and rejected me. The day after that, I went home feeling disappointed and angry, knowing that friendships were fickle.

I internalized everything those kids said and I started to hate my hair, constantly wondering what other people thought of me. I was suspicious of new people, of whether they were really trying to be my friends or just trying to make me a victim again. Going from being popular to a nobody in one day simply because of your hair texture will do that to you.

I never saw that boy again and I hated that he was my first experience with sex. I hated that it wasn't loving and sweet like the movies promised it would be. I hated that I allowed him to have me just because he gave me some snacks. I hated that sex had become meaningless for me, just something to do, after that experience.

Even though it was years before I had sex again, I realize now that I took that attitude about boys and friendships into every relationship I had after that first one. I would have a boyfriend and have sex with him, but would never feel a thing for him. It became easy for me to have detached sexual encounters with men just to get them to shut up about having sex.

When I met my husband, I knew sex with him was different, but it still took me a while to understand that the difference was intimacy and love. Before, I never really felt pleasure from sex and never really looked forward to it. But with my husband I could enjoy it, because this man was here to stay.

It took me accepting what happened on that day as a kid—understanding my reactions to it all and how I allowed it to play out in my adult life, and accepting it all as an experience—to stop judging myself and start loving myself.

Dear Daughter:

What I went through when I made the choice to gain the acceptance of the group of kids I was with taught me that just because people like you, it doesn't mean they have your best interest at heart. You see, that boy had no intention of loving me forever. Shoot, he probably had no intention of even liking me past that one week of vacation. He didn't care about how I would feel or if I would recover from the rejection.

I learned, after quite some time, to make better choices for myself, but more specifically, I learned to never allow myself to go through that type of situation again. I learned to accept myself, but first I had to learn that I was made to be loved. With that, I had to focus on loving myself so I could teach and hold a standard for the people I met. Learning to love myself first was a huge part of that lesson.

I held a grudge against that boy, those kids, and myself for years because I mistook what I did as a flaw in my character. Then I compounded it with more bad choices—until I finally learned to accept it as an isolated incident and not a reflection of who I am as a person. I also learned that people's opinions of me don't define me and that I needed to own my mistakes. See, I chose to have sex that day. I chose to create and continue meaningless relationships. I chose to do the things I did, and I had the power to choose to make wiser decisions. I also had the power to stop my self-destructive behavior and love myself—and I did just that!

I love myself because I am beautiful, inside and out. I define myself as strong, smart, confident, determined, and loving. I love myself and I want you to love yourself and stay true to yourself, flaws and all. When you do that, you empower others to accept and love you as well.

I know how hard it is to be comfortable in your own skin, hair, and body, but learning to accept and approve of my own self-image was the best decision I have ever made. I want you to have that same liberation by approving of yourself and standing on that, no matter what anyone else says about you.

Don't allow your self-esteem, value, or self-approval to be dependent on anything outside of yourself. Shoes, clothes, hair, makeup, jewelry, and cars are all just accessories. They don't define your worth. In fact, you define them. You pick and choose which accessories will compliment you, not which ones will bring value to you. When you stand naked in front of your mirror, you should still be happy with who you see.

As your mother, it is my job to make sure you understand that your body is a temple, meant to be treasured, respected, protected, and loved. Sex is an intimate act that we use our bodies for, and it should be done in a committed union as an act of solidifying love for a lifetime, not as just a moment of fun for someone else. Anyone sharing in your body should cherish you tenderly and wholeheartedly, caring for and loving you.

You are special and should be handled with love and care. Not only are you enough, you are the prize! So, every day, be the best you. Flash your winning smile and extend your hand to people as a sign that you are open to new relationships. Doing so will add value to others and increase your level of influence with them.

I will always love you, no matter what, because you are my baby girl. You can always find refuge and rest here in my heart. Always know that you have me beside you, pushing you to be everything you have dreamed of being and making sure you believe in both yourself and your ability to make things happen. From the day I knew I was pregnant with you, I have stood on this scripture:

> For this reason, since the day we heard about you, we have not stopped praying for you. We continually ask God to fill you with the knowledge of his will through all the wisdom and understanding that the Spirit gives. Colossians 1:9 (NIV)

You were intentionally created and it is such an honor to be your mom.

Journal Page

April Mack

Dear Diary: Running from a Bully Nearly Cost Me Everything

It saddens me when I turn on the television and see stories of how a ten-year-old child has taken their own life after being relentlessly tormented by bullies. Social media and the internet have made this information more readily accessible, and it literally breaks my heart when I log in to my Facebook account and see another news report of someone's baby who felt that hopeless and alone. I understand how they feel because I've been there before. When it was happening to me I had no idea that so many others had faced the same torment that I dealt with for so many years. But, as I'm sure others have found before me, when you're going through crap, you feel like it has only happened to you and that no one else has had it as bad as you did.

Nowadays when people see me, I'm sure they see a very confident and even outspoken woman who is not afraid to stand up for herself. I take great pride in showing my daughters and others how to stand up to bullies. I'm doing my very best to give them practical advice on how to set boundaries and how to recognize and defuse situations where predatory people are trying to take advantage of them. I work hard to ensure that my daughters have a different experience than I had as a child.

Growing up in a single parent household with a mother who was so strong and tough wasn't easy. I can remember my mom always being so doggone busy making a way to provide for me and my younger brother. I can't feel sorry for myself though, because I had it easy compared to her; she was raised by my grandfather and he was hard as nails!

My grandmother's untimely death when my mother was still a child herself took a real toll on my family back then. It pretty much left my grandfather to raise and support a young daughter and a house full of boys on his own. It's easy to see why Mom didn't take crap from anybody! Looking back, it's pretty clear to me why I was so timid and why I struggled with setting boundaries and speaking up for myself. It's because I never really found my voice, being a part of a family with so many strong personalities, and where everyone has a sort of take-charge attitude. It pains me to know how all of those things set me up for being ripe picking for bullies.

The bullying started when I was in elementary school, but I can most vividly remember a time when I was bullied in high school that totally changed my life. I hate how I felt, living that experience, but I am thankful to God for it now because it was the catalyst that aided me in finally finding my voice and it gave me the courage to stand up for myself.

I can't even remember why that girl hated me. I can remember going over our interactions in my mind to see if I had ever done anything to her, and I had not! The bullying with her started in the first semester of my ninth grade school year. I was just like everyone else: nervous, afraid of a new adventure in a new school environment, and so desperate for people to like me. My bully and I shared a world history class, and I vividly recall how every single day she would stare me down. I truly believe that I have a friendly face. I remember giving her this half smile, and in return, this chick just glared at me. I can't forget how she dressed and looked. She wore a low-hanging ponytail that kind of stuck up in the back. She had these mean, piercing eyes that she used to cut me dirty looks. Every single day she wore an all-black windbreaker and some Nike Cortez tennis shoes. I used to hate when our teacher placed us in a group together because that girl would always make a point to let others know how much she hated me. She cut me off when I was talking and she would make these unnecessary, snarky, sarcastic remarks to me.

I can remember one time when I tried to stand up to her, but I failed miserably. Mr. Johnson, our teacher, asked the class a question and I totally knew the answer. I quickly raised my hand and he called on me to answer the question. As soon as I began to talk, though, as if she was on cue, this thang muttered something under her breath. But all I heard was the punch line that involved calling me the "b word." Everyone in the class started to laugh at me, especially her homies. What's worse is that our teacher barely even reprimanded her. In fact, he laughed too! From that day forward, things started to get much worse for me.

One day, after lunch, while we were all waiting for our teacher to let us back in the classroom, I overheard the bully tell her home girl that she was gonna whoop my (you know what) and cut my hair. Of course, she said it loud enough that I, and others, could hear what she said. I was thinking, "Here they go again, laughing at me. I bet they all know that I'm 'scary,' that I'm a wimp." I'm not even going to lie, it sent chills up my spine and I immediately got the bubble guts! I remember thinking, "Lord knows I can't fight and I'm tired of feeling scared every time I see this girl in class. I'm even more tired of ducking out of the cafeteria or gym every time she walks past me. Ugh! I'm about to start ditching this stupid class." That's when I made the decision to ditch that dumb class for real! But once I started ditching that class, I started falling behind in my sixth-period class—so I started ditching that class, too.

It started a chain reaction of me falling behind in my grades and an awful cycle of daily ditching.

I remember reaching out to my mother to discuss what was going on, but she gave me the most awful advice ever. In my mom's world, it was commonplace to fight everyone and everything. Having three older brothers made her a fighter. I recall, one night we were all sitting down eating dinner and I began to use the opportunity to talk to her about the girl at school who was picking on me. But before I could even finish my story, she said, "You just need to punch her in the mouth!" In her opinion, the only way to beat a bully was to walk up to the one with the biggest mouth, and once you sock them, everyone else is going to shut up and leave you alone. Uh, Mom, did I mention that I can't fight? I remember thinking, "Great, I'm doomed." I walked away from that talk already feeling defeated. I didn't feel comfortable talking to anyone at school because I didn't want to be called a snitch, and the only option that was presented to me at home was the advice to fight—and I wasn't comfortable doing that at all.

The first six months of my freshman year in high school was a huge blur, because once I started to ditch class, the days began to blend into one another. My mom would wake me and my younger brother up for school and we would all get dressed and leave at the same time. She would drop me off at the bus stop, but I would either take the bus to the beach or I would simply go back home and sleep until it was late in the afternoon. Looking back, that period of my life was really depressing, and it became what I can only describe as a dreadful cycle of letting myself down over and over again, simply because I refused to be brave and ask for help. Every single day I remember feeling so scared to go to school because someone wanted to fight with me. I was also afraid to stay at home all day because my mom could have come home and caught me. It's hard to believe I did that whole song and dance for so long, just because I was afraid of being called a snitch, a coward, or worse—a buster—by the kids in school if they found out that I told on my bully.

One thing I didn't consider was what would happen if I were caught by someone other than my mom—and that's when things drastically changed for me. One morning, when I was sitting at the bus stop, a police officer pulled up next to me. This was the straw that broke the camel's back and caused my entire situation to be exposed for all to see. I was literally placed into the back of the police car and was given a citation for truancy. My mother was called and informed and they requested that she pick me up from the police station—and she was furious! My mother grounded me for what seemed to be an eternity and she scheduled a conference with my counselor and my teachers. My grades were horrible and there was no time to make up the classes, which meant I had to spend the next three summers in summer school! My mother and I had to appear in court before a judge and I was forced to explain why I missed school. My mom was ordered to pay a fine!

When I got caught ditching it seemed like the worst thing in the world that could ever happen to me, but I see things differently now. Looking back, this was honestly one of the best things that could have happened to me—but it honestly could have all been prevented if I had just reached out for help.

While I was dealing with my mother, my teachers, and my impending court date, I learned that my bully was expelled from the school for fighting. I can't exactly say that I was pleased to hear this news, but I do remember hearing that she was transferred to another school closer to her home, and that did give me some peace. But I know that some kids aren't as lucky as I was. So when I hear the horror stories about the children that end up taking their own lives because of cyberbullying, my stomach immediately sinks. I was a teen that believed there was no end in sight to the relentless bullying. I am so grateful that I did not wind up as a statistic, a person with no hope that chose suicide as the permanent answer to my temporary and very preventable situation.

Dear Daughters:

If you have been bullied in school I know how you feel. This was one of the most frightening experiences I dealt with as a teenager. I understand what it's like to be at an age where you're already struggling with your own self-confidence and with fitting in with your friends, and then, on top of that, you're dealing with someone who wants to make you feel small, someone who wants to make you feel overpowered by them; it can be a daunting experience for anyone.

I really thank God that nothing ever happened to me while I was ditching school, while I rode the public bus all over town, or as I sat at the beach. If someone wanted to do harm to me, my mother would not have known the last place I had been to tell the authorities where to check for me. She wouldn't have known my last whereabouts because she had believed I was at school. I could've gotten seriously hurt by someone who was way more dangerous than the bully girl at school.

Now I'm going to be honest with you. I still have no idea what was going on with that girl, or why she treated me so horribly in school. She could have been a foster child, she could have been dealing with abuse at home, or she could have just had low self-esteem, which caused her to treat me that way. Who knows? What I do know is that you do not have to live in fear of bullies!

No one should ever have to go to school, or any other place, while constantly dealing with the fear that someone will try to crush them verbally, emotionally, physically, spiritually, or in any other way. Bullying can include unwanted teasing, physically touching you against your will, purposely excluding you with the intention of hurting you emotionally and other harassing behaviors. This includes the bully that wants to take your personal items against your will, the jerk that wants to call you hurtful names, and even the tough guy or girl that thinks it's cool to threaten you with physical harm. If you believe that you or someone you know is being bullied, you must take action. You are not alone and you aren't helpless. Many of us have gone through the same experience as you and there are people out here that will help you. Whatever you do, please don't do like I did and begin to ditch school. And above all else, please don't harm yourself. There are resources out there to help you, and they will help you put an end to the bullying you are experiencing.

I know that sometimes it can be hard to talk to me or to other people you love about things like this because you think you've let us down or don't want to bother us. Never think that you've let us down! But even if you can't bring yourself to ask me or someone else in our family for help, don't let that stop you from getting help! If you don't feel comfortable talking to your friends or classmates, you can reach out to a teacher, counselor, or other school administrators. Another option is to find an adult that you can trust that will have your back and will help you with taking action. The police are an available resource as well. Please remember, running from the situation, taking matters into your own hands by fighting, and ditching school all have consequences of their own. Bullying is a crime in most states and there are people out there that will help you. The bottom line is this: bullying should not be tolerated and you, dear daughters, do not have to put up with it!

Journal Page

Ashley Shaw

Dear Diary: Sometimes Danger Lurks Instead of Fun

One year when I was in my late twenties, I flew from Los Angeles to Atlanta to visit my family and some friends. It was ten years after I graduated from high school and I was excited that the Mays High ten year reunion festivities happened to land on the weekend I was in town. Even though I didn't graduate from Mays because of my move back to Cali in my junior year, I couldn't wait to pop in to some of the reunion events and see my old friends.

I didn't have a ticket to the reunion event, but when has that ever stopped me? I headed out to see if I could either sneak in or meet up with a few people outside of the venue. After refusing to pay the $50 entry fee, I got a chance to hang out with about fifteen long-time friends in the area adjacent to the front door for a short period of time. Because the night was still young, I decided to go to a nightclub with my girls KK and CC, along with another friend of theirs. Four young women in their late twenties out for a fun girls' night out. Nothing special, nothing that I hadn't done hundreds of times before. We caught up for a bit and, after hitting the dance floor, we headed to the bar to get drinks. The bar was a smaller, stand-alone bar and the bartender worked for the establishment. We were literally standing right next to the bar while the drinks were made, just talking and having a great time. The bartender seemed friendly and made a little small talk as he made the drinks. We paid and left the bar area to finish the night.

Because I was driving, I limited myself to one drink at the beginning of the night, knowing I would be dancing, sweating it out on the dance floor, and drinking water for at least the next two to three hours and that my driving wouldn't be impaired. I followed all of the steps and necessary precautions I usually took to ensure a safe, fun night. At that point there were no red flags; nothing seemed out of the ordinary and everyone was happy, having a fun night, and enjoying each other's company.

When it was time to leave, as we were walking to the car, I turned to my friend KK and said, "Ugh, I don't feel so good." As I sat in the driver's seat I immediately leaned over and threw up next to the car. Almost instantaneously my head felt extremely heavy, and I felt as if it was too heavy to lift up. I looked in my friend's direction and she half turned to me with her eyes closed. She told me that she didn't feel good either. I let out a huge sigh and asked her if she was well enough to give me directions to get back to my parents' house. She said she could, and at that point everything else gets extremely foggy.

All I remember on the drive home was feeling as if my head weighed fifty pounds, and that I was fighting to use the steering wheel to hold my head up. It took all of my energy to peek over the dashboard. I have no idea how long it took us to get home and I felt like I was driving at ten mph.

I don't remember getting home or walking into the house, or how my friend was able to get home.

When we talked in the morning and debriefed about the night, we quickly realized that something had been put into our drinks. The first reaction was comical: girl—someone tried to get us . . . people really still do that? But as I made call after call, checking on everyone and attempting to piece back together memories that didn't exist, it became more and more sobering. To top that, one of my friends since middle school, who I ran into at the reunion event prior to going to the club, called me to make sure I was alright. Apparently, in my half-consciousness I called him to try to get help because I knew he and some other friends had been in the area earlier in the night, but he said I had been so incoherent that he hadn't been sure what I was saying. That was sobering and literally stopped me in my tracks.

Dear Daughter:

I want to start by looking at the bigger picture of what happened to me and asking some basic questions: What if something had happened? What if KK hadn't been coherent enough to give me the directions back to the house? It was a blessing that we made it home safely. I could have lost my license or my career—or, even worse, injured or even killed myself or someone else.

Writing this to you almost a decade later, the realization is even scarier than it was in the moment. Even now, recalling that night, there are complete holes that I have tried to fill by piecing the night back together, but haven't been able to. There is a major difference between forgetting what happened and being given a substance that completely and involuntarily left irretrievable absences of large chunks of memory.

I thought that, at twenty-eight years old, I knew everything I needed to know, and never in a thousand years would I have thought that such a thing would happen to me. I knew all of the rules: never let someone you don't know hand you a drink, don't leave your drink unattended... I got the drink directly from the bartender and so I must have been safe. Right? Apparently not. The one key rule we did follow, and which ultimately saved us, is to ALWAYS keep an eye on and stick close to the people you are with and to leave with who you came with. We stuck together like a pack and had *so* much fun, and if somebody thought they were gonna catch us slipping, unfortunately for them and fortunately for us—they picked the wrong group of women.

What I learned about myself was that I was getting over-confident with being an "adult." Yes, I was on my own and self-sufficient in life and lifestyle, but that didn't exempt me from something potentially happening to me. No matter how careful and able to take care of myself I thought I was, I still fell victim to a sick, twisted person. Even being 100 percent vigilant and prepared, things can happen in the blink of an eye. I needed to be more humble and respectful of life and to realize that me being responsible and a good person didn't exempt me from the actions of bad people. For as much as I had lived through and experienced in life, there was so much more that I didn't know. And that's what really showed me that I TRULY had no idea how much I didn't know.

The first thing I want you to know and ALWAYS remember is that you don't have to feel like you're stuck and need help but are on your own. Although I did attempt to phone another friend in my fog of attempting to be responsible, my first call should have been to my true support system in the equation . . . my parents. At the time, I didn't want to call my parents as there was a level of embarrassment that I had gotten caught in that predicament, even though it was not a result of being reckless or wild. However, my bigger issue is that it was hard to ask my parents for help, because I had been let down by both of them in the past.

Although I know that the whole situation was a big deal and I could and should have made a call to my parents my first option, I had been conditioned to have a constant feeling that I was on my own. I felt I was not truly supported and had to fend for myself. Although not intentional, that feeling was and still is constantly bolstered by statements from all of my parents, which are generally expressed as "you are smart, responsible, and resourceful, and you are the one (kid) we never had to worry about." I was an "easy" kid, extremely independent, and didn't require much supervision or garner negative attention. Coupled with being the oldest of my siblings, I became a pseudo-parent and -adult while I was still in adolescence and, in many ways, began the process of raising myself. As a child of divorce since age one, I had moved between parents for as long as I can remember. I was always going back and forth and never felt a solid sense of belonging at either home. I could tell you hundreds of stories of how this feeling was built up over the years, but it solidified during an incident when my car broke down on the side of the freeway late at night. I called my father to come get me, but after they tried loading the rest of the family in the car a decision was made—and I got a call back telling me to call my mechanic and see if he would come get me. Because I never fully felt like I could trust my parents to help me if I needed, it manifested into difficulty truly trusting anyone close to me, which resulted in my not asking for help when we were drugged.

By the grace of God, everything and everyone turned out fine during that night out, but I want you to know that you do not have to feel like you can only rely on friends, or worse, strangers, when you feel your back is up against a wall. There is a principle known as "repeat or repair," that you must learn from your mistakes or be doomed to repeat them. My job is to make sure that I break the cycle of having children that feel isolated or abandoned. I want you know and truly feel, beyond a shadow of a doubt, that you are loved and supported, and that no matter what happens you have a support system to turn to. My goal every day is to show you how to navigate through life and to help you understand that you do not have to walk through life feeling alone.

There are good people out there, but not everyone who smiles at you is a friend, and people may have sick, twisted reasons behind their actions toward you. In this situation, why did we get drugged? Someone had to be a sick individual to do that, to participate in and to help facilitate trying to take advantage of us and who knows how many others. Even if you do all you can do to be vigilant and responsible, you are still open to being taken advantage of and being hurt. Do not harden your heart and do not give up on people, but always make sure you are alert, coherent, and in general have a safety plan. And never feel like you don't have a support system or can't turn to them for fear of embarrassment or reprimand. Be honest, and know that we have also lived life and seen A LOT of things that you would probably be shocked to hear.

Even with that, there will come a time when your dad and I will not be around to help or save you. It's important that you always stay responsible and watch out for yourself and the other people you are with if you go out in a group. Make sure that you stay coherent under your own power. Don't even get sloppy drunk, and if you are the designated driver, make sure you are completely sober. Stay with the group and do not allow anyone to be left behind. Make sure you are in contact or proximity with your people. You never know who the predators are, and they could come in any form. Finally, leave with who you came with. I have met plenty of nice people while I was out, and have actually been friends with them for years and even decades. But anyone interested in dating you and taking you home most likely isn't interested in a friendship. And if they are, or even if they want to possibly become friends with benefits, there is NO reason that those conversations can't be had over the course of the next day, week, or month. Everyone seems more interesting with alcohol in their (or your) system, and when you get them in the true light of day and see them for who they truly are, your opinion may GREATLY change.

The main point that I want you to take away, even if you don't get anything else, is this: if one of us had truly been the designated driver and abstained from drinking completely, we would never have been in that situation. If you can't have fun with your friends without a drink being involved, then you need new friends. No matter what kind of pressure may be put on you, no drink is worth risking your life. It's your responsibility to be responsible. If no one else is willing to not drink when you go out, then YOU step up and be that person. Otherwise, choose to stay at the house and drink, and plan to spend the night, use Uber, or get a ride home. There are so many opportunities in your life to go out. None are worth risking or losing your life.

So, my dear daughter, I wish I had a lifetime to tell you my stories, shield you from all pain and harm, and protect you from all dangers, seen and unseen. But I can't. I want you to truly live your life, and do so without the constraints of thinking you have to conform with the norm or live the life you think your parents would want you to live. Please follow your heart, but do so by making good and informed decisions, and be the best person that you can be. You will win, lose, love, be loved by, hurt, and be hurt by other people, and my prayer for you is that you always seek to do and be your best, never injure anyone on purpose, and live a full and happy life—and learn from my mistakes so you don't have to make them yourself.

I love you and love all of you reading this. Go forward and be great!

Journal Page

Dee French

Dear Diary: Don't Forget to Breathe

I remember being a young eighteen-year-old girl who loved to laugh and hang out with my friends. I would go to work and college, and I made enough money to take care of myself. I would dance for hours and travel, just wanting to explore all over. I was very stylish, with all the newest outfits, and loved to keep myself beautifully dressed. Everyone asked me where I shopped, so I eventually started shopping for others as an extra job. But then things started to change.

The neighborhood we lived in started to get dangerous. It seemed like every week somebody was getting shot; some of my family members had passed away due to the danger of that community. My family needed to move, so I got two jobs to help my parents buy a house to move into. This was a great thing, helping my family, and I started helping others, too.

However, as I got older I had a strong desire to help everyone in need and didn't understand balance.

All the kids loved to hang at my new house, and I even started working in the community, giving to the needy. I had kids and got married, even bought a second house; everything was great. But little by little I was giving more of my time away, and I stopped doing the things I loved, all to help others. Was it a good idea to allow me to put everyone else first? I acted just like I did as a child when I jumped rope with my friends, always letting everyone else have my turn.

After my dad died, I became depressed and started making choices that would let me focus on others in order to not deal with the loss and pain I felt. I avoided dealing with my reality by doing more things for the community, the church, and the people, instead of taking time to heal. It is good to love doing all these things, but it is essential to know when we need to be healed from the issues in our lives. Too often, though, we learn to smile and function when we really want to cry. When did putting a mask over our face to cover our real feelings become the standard way to live? Suffering in silence is not the way God wants us to live, but this is what shame does to us. It makes us feel that nobody cares about our concerns or heart matters. Learning to function or live without dealing with the issues of your heart is not healthy, and it all will eventually flow out. Proverbs 4:23 states, "Above all else, guard your heart, for everything you do flows from it."

Even if you don't say anything, at some point the issues you don't deal with will begin to show. It is essential that you love yourself and be bold about enjoying life on your terms.

As I am writing this today, I remember how I came to realize that my kids were concerned for me and wondered if I was really happy. My kids wanted to see their mom, see me, hang with my friends and laugh like I used to, before I thought that the only thing I could be was their mom. It seemed like I gave my whole life over for my kids and everyone else. I even stayed in a marriage that I wasn't happy in for my kids. I wanted to help, to save the world, but while I was helping I forgot to take care of myself. I forgot to breathe. I had loved to travel, dance, and laugh, but somehow all my dreams were set aside to help others.

This was difficult for me, realizing that I stayed in my marriage not out of love, but for others' happiness, and put myself last in so many areas. Instead I thought of others, like my kids, intent on keeping up the image and always helping anyone who needed help. You never want to stay in a relationship that doesn't make you happy or give you great joy. It was a hard decision, but I looked at my kids and thought of them, so I stayed. It's embarrassing to me now because I allowed myself to get lost in the desire to keep my family together. When you are in a relationship or marriage, it should be that you want to stay, because you and your spouse or mate are both in love with each other.

Do not allow other people or your emotions to define your decisions. You need to have a clear mind when you make life-changing decisions that will affect you. You don't have to rush; it's okay if you need more time to get your thoughts together. Remember that your choices, whether right or wrong, can have consequences. However, it is okay if you need to fix or change the direction you wanted to go in.

I learned it was possible to help others and still live a fulfilled life. I could live out any dream I had put on hold to raise my family or had allowed to slip by, all while still helping others live their dreams. When I first went into business, I needed to clearly write down what I wanted for my business, relationships, and desires. This ensured that for any choice I make, I have a guide to follow and refer to, so I don't compromise beyond what I can afford to. I learned to apply that to every part of my life.

I learned self-care and that it's okay to say no. Saying no doesn't make you mean or uncaring, it just means that you learned boundaries. I now like to make time for myself; to pamper myself and not let anyone invade my space; and to allow God to revive, restore, and reinvent me so I can live the life that I love on my terms, not the terms others set for me. I have also learned to accept help when it comes. I used to say, "oh, no, you don't have to," thinking it was a burden to others and that I didn't want to put more on them. But helping others goes both ways; it's not just one-sided. I have learned to accept it and know it doesn't make me weak; rather, it makes me strong, because I know my limits. I am learning more about myself every day and loving the person the Holy Spirit is growing me to be.

Dear Daughter:

You are beautifully and wonderfully made! Live your life on your terms and always take care of yourself, knowing that God has the answer to everything. Write down your goals in detail so you know what it takes to get there. Also, never get so busy that you don't take time to breathe. Schedule in time for yourself and never let anyone invade that space. This gives you time to regroup, relax, and get clarity on your next decision for your business, life, or family.

Always know your values and stand up for what you believe in, no matter what. Knowing your values will ensure you never compromise them and that you will make choices that you are comfortable with. Respect yourself first! Continue to carry yourself in a respectful manner and never let anyone disrespect you, not your family, somebody you are dating, or anyone else. Make sure you bring to order anybody that disrespects you, and if he or she doesn't change after you speak to them about it, then you must remove yourself from them and reduce the impact they have in your life. Be wise in the people you choose to be around. Try to be around people that are confident enough to challenge you, so you can view things differently, too, not just from your perspective. You are very precious and should be treated like a queen.

You are a queen and will have guys interested in seeing you. So, don't fall in love with the first person that says something nice to you. You were validated at home and know who you are and that you are beautifully and wonderfully made. When somebody else says it, it won't be a shock, but a compliment. I want you to know that you are already complete just the way you are. The love you seek is already inside you, because you must love yourself first. Remember, it is very special when two people love each other, and the moments they share can feel like a lifetime. Therefore, it is important to love yourself first so you can show others what you love. You are a fantastic person, and it is sure that you will also attract amazing people, so I know you will be found by the one that you can share your love with. In the meantime, love yourself and get to know you.

I must mention sex because it is part of life, but I will encourage you to wait until you get married to share this special part of yourself. So, let me share some differences about sex. Sex and romance are both beautiful things, but you must be careful, as they are not the same as love. The feeling of a kiss or a hug, or going on a first date, can run through your entire body, making you think you're in love. But it may just be chemistry with someone you really like. When true love is experienced by two people, it is warm, kind, and seems endless.

The love that never dies, the love where, even when mistakes are made, they love you anyway—that is the love I want for you, the love that lasts for a lifetime.

You should also remember that love is kind and is shown through the way you treat everyone. As you grow, you will forget many things you did in the past. You won't remember the things you thought were important in high school or college; you won't remember every crush you had. However, you will remember those that were kind and loved you when you needed someone to talk with. These are the people that can be friends for a lifetime, so cherish the ones that love you and show you kindness.

I am always here to listen when you need me. So, live a life that you are proud of, and remember, it is never too late to change your mind and do the things you really want and love. I have always been your greatest supporter, your biggest fan, and have loved you since the moment I found out I was pregnant. I believe in you and nothing can ever change that; you know I will never give up on you, and I will always be there to cheer you on. As my daughter, you reminded me that I have my own life as well and that I have permission to enjoy it. You are so smart, and I thank you for sharing this with me.

You have a good brain, so use it. Think for yourself and don't allow peer pressure to make you choose something you are not comfortable with. It is okay to say NO. As parents, we can guide our children by helping them with decisions, but we should never make you feel that you can't make your own choices. We will always have your best interests at heart, so please know that we are not trying to control you, we just want you to be okay. If you make a mistake, admit it so you can learn from the lesson it will give you. Even as adults we struggle with owning up when we make mistakes and sometimes repeat the same errors. The lesson is to learn from your mistakes and not to be too hard on yourself when you make them. You are very talented and good at many things, so learn from the mistakes and move on with your life.

Earlier I mentioned knowing your values in life and in business. Keeping this in mind will help you define your own success and what it means to you, so that it is defined by what you want and not by what you see others doing. You can create your own success story; I believe in you. God has made just one you, and everything about you is different. You are unique, and never think for one minute that you must live up to what other people want you to be. Live boldly and love it. Love being who you were created to be; you are awesome. Enjoy what you do; this is your life, and you only have one, so give it everything you have and have no regrets. Let the world see just how wonderful you are, and take it by storm! You are a voice that needs to be heard; never let anyone keep you quiet. Grow in grace and learn to use your words healthily with effective communication skills that show the best you. Words are very powerful; they can uplift, build, and tear down, so choose them wisely, and never let anybody try to bring you down with negative words. You are precious and valuable and should be treated like a queen every time.

Lastly, and importantly, be financially independent, making sure you have your own money. Handle money wisely and use what you were taught to make good decisions. When you go to a store or mall, before you begin buying everything you see, you need to ask yourself if you need to buy it. You don't want to waste money on things that will fade away or not grow in value. Yes, it is okay to want wonderful things, but never overdo it; remember the rules of money management. Pay your 10 percent tithes and 10 percent to yourself for the future, then pay your bills and put spending money aside to buy the stuff you love.

This chapter is a guide for you, my precious daughter, and there is so much more I could say. Just remember: in everything you do, don't forget to love life! Stay passionate about living a fulfilling life that brings you extraordinary joy, creating memories that will last a lifetime—and journal as you go so your children can read it. You have everything you need inside of you; remember, no regrets. Live, laugh, love, and leave a legacy that you will be proud of. Love you always.

Journal Page

Ereena George

Dear Diary: Ugly Feet Made Me Dislike Myself

I really wish my aunt would have never told me that my feet were ugly. Her words really skewed the way I viewed myself for the next nine years of my life. From age eight to seventeen I hated my feet. It's funny how something as unimportant as my feet could affect my entire youth and start a downward spiral of how I would treat myself and have others treat me.

I never wanted to wear open toe shoes when I was young; I wore sneakers a lot, which is probably why my feet are so big (at least that's what I've been told.) It didn't matter to me, though, I did not care; all I knew was that no one was going to see my toes as long as I could help it.

It wasn't until I was in high school that I realized the hate for my feet had grown into something bigger, that I hated everything about me. My hair was too short, I was fat, and, more than anything else, my skin was too dark, and no one liked dark skin. The dislike I had for myself is what caused my depression as a teenager; it was also the reason I allowed people to treat me however they wanted, good or bad.

My plan to keep anyone from seeing my toes worked out just fine until senior prom. My intention was to not attend my senior prom. I wasn't at all interested in the concept of having to wear a dress and open toe shoes; pair that with the fact that I didn't have a date, it was a no go—but I allowed my friends to convince me and so I went.

I had to do an exhausting amount of mental work in order to convince myself that it was okay to show my toes. For weeks I looked at my feet, painted my toenails, took the polish off, painted them again. I would look at my siblings' feet to see if they looked as bad as mine; I looked at my mother's feet, my friends' feet, anyone's feet. It was like an obsession to figure out if my feet were good enough to be out in the open. I wasn't convinced at all, but I still went with it.

I will never forget the day of my prom. I wore an ice-blue dress, a white feather boa, and white open toe shoes . . . with white stockings. It probably would have looked better if I hadn't worn stockings, but I could not convince myself to leave my feet bare; all of my work and self-talk did nothing to erase the nine years where I allowed myself to internalize my aunt's words. As I stood in front of the mirror looking at the woman I was becoming, everything I had experienced ran through my mind. It's funny how, when you place yourself in situations that make you uncomfortable, you begin to think about everything else as well.

It was a beautiful day out, as sunny as it could be. The limo was coming to pick me up first. All of my neighbors were outside as usual, but you couldn't tell me that they were not out there to see me, to see my feet. I tried all that I could to stay in as long as possible, but I could stall no more. My feet walked out of the front door onto the porch and into the world for all to see; no longer could I or would I hide them in shame—I left that for other parts of my life.

The prom was wonderful; there's nothing better than hanging out with friends, dancing and having fun. It was truly a night to remember, because no one noticed my feet. I believe that that was the first time I received compliments from my peers; I never knew how much I needed them until it happened. "Ereena, you look so good." "Wow, I can't believe you wore a dress and shoes." "Your hair looks really nice." They were simple words that had never been uttered to me before. For so many years I walked around not hearing good things about myself, so much so that I chose to live with all of the negativity. Even when it came to dating, I always wondered why boys would even approach me; where was the attraction? It didn't make much of a difference—I dated them anyway— but my choices were based on how I thought about myself at the time; needless to say, those choices were not good. I found myself talking to boys that I didn't even find attractive, kissing boys that I didn't like, and placing myself in very uncomfortable situations.

Ugly feet caused 45 percent of my low self-esteem; mental and physical abuse took care of the rest. I was so happy when people chose to talk to me or be my friend. I didn't care what they were into, what they liked, or how much trouble we might get in, I just wanted to be around people that (I thought) truly liked me. It's funny how, when you don't set boundaries for yourself or your life, people pick up on that and use it to their advantage. Although I was very mature for my age, there were many things I did not know about relationships of all kinds, which made me very susceptible to being used, especially by family. Thinking that my family loved me no matter what, I would do anything for them, even if it made me uncomfortable. I always said yes because I just knew that one day, when I needed them, they would reciprocate—boy was I wrong. In order for people to reciprocate they have to care about you and your feelings; when they only care about their feelings, they figure out ways to play you against yourself and you don't even know it. In my case, my family knew that I loved food and that if you offered me a meal for a favor I would do it. Yes, it kept me unhealthy, but food was my coping mechanism and the only thing that made me feel wanted and normal.

After I got through prom I knew that I wanted something different for my life. I no longer wanted to hide my toes or myself from anyone. I knew that in order to change my life I needed to change my way of thinking; it took some convincing, but it worked. My first step was looking in the mirror every day and convincing myself that other people's opinions of me did not matter, that my skin was beautiful and my body would be what I made it. I worked on this every day, more so when I was in school; through my healing I realized that having peers around was not good for my self-esteem because I constantly compared myself to them. Any time I was alone I would say these words in my head: "You are somebody and people are only going to love you if you love yourself first." It was a secret healing, something I shared with no one, not even family, because they were dangerous to my healing process.

Working provided me the opportunity to buy my own shoes, and one of my first purchases was a pair of open toe sandals. Was I super excited to put them on? No. Did I know that I needed to wear them as part of my healing? Yes. In no way, shape, or form was it easy; people would look at my feet and ask "Why do they look like that? Why is your toe on top of the next one?" Every time someone would mention my feet I would have to start the healing process over again because I still felt uncomfortable about my feet. It would take me three to four years to finally be happy with my feet and myself in general. It finally happened because I had done the work—but also because the universe provided me with the opportunity to discover that my aunt had placed her own insecurities on me.

There was a family BBQ one June; everyone was in attendance, including my aunt. Everyone had on their open toe shoes as we mingled, ate, and listened to music. At one point during the day I just so happened to look down at my aunt's feet. I was mortified! Her feet were so ugly, really ugly and hairy. I could not stop staring; I looked over each toe as if I worked for forensics and was reviewing a crime scene. Each corn, each hair, and each bend made me smile. I wasn't even aware that I was smiling until someone asked what I was smiling for. The question brought me back; I found a seat in the corner and my entire childhood ran through my mind. I wanted to slap my aunt for ruining me with her words and causing me to hate myself, but I didn't. I sat and smiled. I could finally walk out of my house without being concerned about what people would think or say to me.

Now, you may be thinking, "Wow, that's excellent." However, I may have gotten over the feelings, but always being on the defensive had turned me into a different person, a mean person. I learned the art of shutting people down and cutting them off! It felt like it was my job to get the last word in every argument or debate; once I realized that I had something special inside of me, I used it for all of the wrong reasons. I cursed people out all of the time if they even thought about looking at me wrong; if I believed there was any kind of injustice going on, I spoke up for myself and everyone else. I thought I was empowered, but I was in pain, deeper pain than I could even imagine at the time. The bullied became the bully.

It's funny how people's perception of me changed when I went from this nice little girl to a defensive, mean teenager and young adult. I had been used for so long that my niceness turned into NO for everything. I refused to help people and would only think about myself. I did not see a problem with that; however, the people around me did not like it at all. I wasn't surprised, because those were the same people who were using me when I was open and willing to help them; a shift in my attitude meant I would no longer accept their treatment, which also meant our relationships were about to fall apart. Some people are not in your life to benefit you; their sole purpose is to benefit themselves. One of the most important lessons I learned from my feet is that I must love myself first and everything else will fall into place.

Dear Daughter:

Don't allow me or anyone else to determine who you are or will be as a person. Some people walk around their entire lives in pain; they learn the art of manipulation and choose to inflict that pain upon others. If you do not take it upon yourself to discover who you are and make the early decision to love yourself regardless of what's being thrown your way, you will get caught up, trapped, and sunken. Trapped with people you hate, including yourself, caught in situations that have nothing to do with you, and sunken into a place so deep you will have no clue how to get out.

I was that person who allowed others to dictate who I am by how they treated me. I walked around in silence and pain for many years, sure of nothing in my life unless someone offered it to me, all because of feet. Not everyone you encounter in your journey is going to be who you think they are; even family will disappoint you at times. You must be mindful of what you allow in your psyche.

We have these conversations all the time; you know that you are worthy, you know that you are loved, that you are beautiful, and above all else you fully understand that you are being raised to be a queen. There are three beliefs that you must carry with you wholeheartedly in order to sit comfortably on your throne:

1. It has been handed to you by a queen.—How could I guide you through this journey, teach you the lessons and provide you with the tools of a queen, if I had not walked the journey myself? Not all journeys are built the same; some roads are full of potholes while others have just been paved. But regardless of the circumstances you start with, they can both yield the same results.

2. You have earned it.—This is the simplest one, because the most important way to earn it is by loving yourself first, all of you, even your flaws, and being able to accept that which you cannot change, yet working daily on what can be improved.

3. You deserve it.—Treat yourself accordingly, by not allowing others to mistreat, abuse, or disrespect you; more importantly, don't do those things to yourself. Self-inflicted wounds hurt the worst and take the longest to heal because there's no one else to blame but yourself. If you lack resources and guidance, self-blame will turn into self-shame.

I know that life is not a fairytale, but queens do exist—and you are currently in training. You are the second generation of cycle breakers; it began with me. The crown you are being given used to be heavy, but my work has lightened the load for you. Take my experience, lessons, and guidance, incorporate it into your own life, and use what works for you. Find new paths on this journey; eventually you will be given the opportunity to place your crown on someone else's head—and when you do, we want it to be as light as a feather.

Journal Page

Ginea Love

Dear Diary: God's Plan Is Still in Full Effect

As I reflect back over my life, I can think of plenty of times when I questioned where my life was headed, especially when I experienced what seemed to be an unexpected life change. One of the most memorable times was when I found out that I was pregnant with my first child at the age of fifteen.

I remember that day like it was yesterday; I had been sick for three days straight from what I was sure was just food poisoning, although my mom didn't believe me. On the third day she decided that we were going to the hospital to get a pregnancy test done. I can still see myself laying in the hospital bed with a gown on, waiting for the doctor to come back with the results of all the tests they ran. I tried to talk to my mom about all of the good things I had going on in school as we passed time, and she would listen and respond, but I could tell she was worried. Every time it would get silent in the room she would whisper to herself, "I hope you aren't pregnant," or something else to that effect. Finally, after what felt like hours of waiting, the doctor came back in the room with the results. It turned out that I didn't just have food poisoning, I was also pregnant. I will never forget the look of disappointment on my mom's face. You see, growing up, I was the one that everyone looked forward to sending to college. My family would always tell me how smart I was and how proud they were of my grades in school. On that day, however, all I could feel coming from my mom was disappointment.

Eventually, life went on; I attended high school, I played sports, and I was on the student council even after my daughter was born. At the same time, however, I was living with my child's father, who was verbally abusing me every day. Every day he would pick me up from school and tell me how stupid I was and how I was never going to be anything. Every day I would get back up, get my daughter ready for daycare, and head to school—but at the end of the day the verbal abuse would start all over again.

A few months after giving birth to my oldest daughter, who I named Alana, I found out that I was pregnant again, with Genise. It was unplanned, and I could sense the disappointment from everyone that I would get pregnant again, especially so soon after giving birth. I even remember someone saying, "Don't be like Ginca; look at her, she got pregnant in high school and now her life will never be the same."

My kid's father and I eventually broke up while I was pregnant the second time. He assaulted me one day and I decided that enough was enough. That day my best friend's sister came to pick me up; I gathered all of my things and the baby's things, got in the car, and never looked back. I moved in with her and her three kids in a one bedroom apartment. I gave birth to my second daughter two weeks before senior prom—and yes, I did go to prom. About a month later I graduated from high school; looking back, it feels good to know that I proved the naysayers wrong, but at the same time I was never trying to prove myself. I never doubted that I was going to graduate high school and go to college, because it was what I was told all my life; it was just a matter of reevaluating the plan.

After graduating high school with the help of my friends and family, I was able to get my own place and start working. At one point in time I was even working two jobs to provide for my girls. I tried going to college for a semester, but it was hard being a single parent with no car, even with all of the support I received from others. I would have to wake up in the morning, get my kids dressed, catch the bus to the sitter's house, drop them off, and catch the bus to school; then, during my lunch break, I would catch the bus to go get the kids and take them to another sitter's house, then catch the bus back to school, and when school was over I would catch the bus to pick up the kids and then we would ride the bus home. It was definitely not the college experience that I was hoping for.

After that first semester I decided to go to a trade school to become an apartment leasing agent. I went to that school for about a month, and after I graduated my sister was able to help me find a job. I remember that I would have to wake up early in the morning and go to the bus stop so that I could drop the girls off at daycare before work. Genise, my second oldest daughter, would make me laugh, because she would always say, "Mommy, we should be sleeping, it's dark outside." At the time I had already started my paperwork to join the Air Force, so I knew it wouldn't be long before things would be different for us. I had always said that I would never join the military, but at that moment in my life as a single parent, trying to make ends meet and with no car, the military sounded pretty good. Plus, they would pay for my college and I would have a dependable job to provide for my girls. Twelve years later, today, I am still in the military and my girls are now the same ages I was when I gave birth to them.

Dear Daughters:

The truth is that disappointments can be hard to accept. I look back at the picture of me at my first baby shower when I was fifteen years old and it amazes me how young I looked. My eyes were bright and full of excitement and my cheeks were a bit chubby and round. I looked like I was playing a game at someone else's baby shower, but instead I was the guest of honor. As a mother myself, I don't even want to try to imagine what my mom felt during that moment in the hospital when the doctor revealed that I was pregnant. Earlier I used the word disappointment, but I'm sure she could think of a few other words to describe how she felt at that moment, such as hurt or sad. But the thing that we have to realize is that a disappointment does not mean the end of God's love for us or his plan for our lives. Although I am not proud of what happened, I don't look at my past with regret; what I have learned is that no matter what happens, God's plan for your life is still in full effect. God has the ability to turn around what may seem like the end of the world to work in your favor. At the time things were hard, but I have always considered you, my daughters, to be my greatest blessing. I now look back at my life and think about how everything just seemed to fall in place at the right time—but during that time I didn't understand it and it felt like things were out of control. One thing is sure, God is always in control. I can't think of a time when I felt alone, even as a single parent, because God sent people to stand in the gap. I have always had strong people, especially strong women, around me to help me along the way, and I am thankful for that. I think that my experiences have not only made me stronger but have also pushed me to want more for you. I try to be everything for you that I felt I needed at your age, and I want to see you succeed.

Another important lesson that I learned was that whether good or bad, our decisions shape our lives; it is important not only to make good decisions, but also to understand why you think and behave the way you do. Understanding what you're up against is half the battle; actually taking action to do better is the other half. A lot of the time, people will find themselves in a negative cycle, and either they don't know it or they can't figure out how to get out of it. That is because they haven't taken the time to figure out the root cause. People don't just act; there is usually a motivation behind our actions. This is important because one decision can change your whole life. Before I got pregnant, my plan was to attend an all-girls college in Pennsylvania and study psychology, but one night of intimacy changed my plans.

I learned that when you are a child your parents stress the importance of making good grades to be successful in life, but you also have to be able to "pass the test" in other areas of your life. While I was good academically and I was never a bad child, that one decision was enough to make a lasting impact. My college experience was nothing like I thought it would be; I didn't plan to attend community college in my hometown. I always dreamed of getting married and having a family with my husband, but instead I was a single parent. The decision I made to join the military was also a life changer, but for the better. I haven't traveled the world just yet, but I have met some great people and I have been able to go to college and provide you girls with a life that I am proud of. These days

I am a lot more cognizant of the decisions that I make. I had to learn this lesson the hard way, and it is my desire to share with you the lessons that I have learned in order to spare you from the heartache of dealing with negative consequences.

I also learned that people don't validate who you are, God does, and he has already given you his stamp of approval. Some people have a way of making your low point feel lower than what it really is. I thank God that I was able to block out the noise and keep moving forward, but it still hurts to be looked down on by others. I struggled with feeling like I failed my family, especially when things didn't work out between me and your father. I was not just a teen parent; I was also a single parent and a statistic. I may have found myself in a less-than-desirable situation, but I had to come to the realization that God still loved me and that I was still worthy.

We are all human beings full of imperfections. While we may not share the same life experiences, that doesn't make the next person any better or worse than us; they just are who they are. You have to learn to love yourself first and foremost and block out all of the negativity. One thing that my mom said that day in the hospital that I will never forget is that "It's already done, we can't sit here and cry about what happened; we have to move forward." I can't even begin telling you how that one sentence has carried me throughout my life. Whenever I found myself in a situation that seemed uncertain, I just kept moving forward. Most times I felt like I didn't have a choice but to keep moving forward, because you girls were depending on me—but also because I refused to quit. I have gone through times where I prayed that God would give me strength because I was weak and I felt like I just couldn't do it anymore, but I just kept on going. I now realize that, during my times of weakness, that is when I was the strongest. I believe that you girls will do great things in this lifetime, but they will not come without adversity. Love yourself as much as possible, speak positive words over yourself, be encouraged, and when times get tough don't give up.

I know I can be hard on you when you do something wrong, but it's only because I want the best for you and I don't want you to have to experience what I went through. I want you to know that, no matter what happens, I am proud of you, but I also want you to take time to find out who you are and to embrace whose you are, a child of the most high God. This includes taking time to get to know your likes and dislikes and striving to fall in love with yourself. Not in an overconfident or selfish way, but in a way where your own happiness is a priority. This is important because happiness is an inside job; you have to take ownership of your life and your own happiness. A lot of times sex, alcohol, and drugs are used to fill voids that people have in their lives. Instead of addressing the issues that are causing them to feel empty and unhappy, they look for ways to feel better by using outside means. What ends up happening is that they make bad decisions and end up feeling worse about themselves.

You have everything you need already inside of you to be happy. You don't have to wait for your joy, you don't need a relationship to have joy, and you don't need material things to be happy; it's already inside of you. If something isn't good for you, be willing to let that thing go; you are worthy of good things in your life. This includes not allowing people to disrespect you and, more importantly, not doing things to disrespect yourself. Furthermore, no matter what anyone has to say about you, as long as you are happy with yourself, that is all that matters. I believe that you should constantly strive to be the best version of yourself, for yourself and no one else. Finally, sometimes life will throw you a curve ball and you will have to curve with it. I want you to know that, no matter what life throws your way, you can overcome it. In life you will make mistakes, but recovering from them is not about the size of the mistake or the number of mistakes, it's about what you do afterward. You just have to acknowledge your mistake, learn from it, pick yourself up, and keep going. Don't ever think a setback is a cause to sit down—it is just a setup for something better. God's plan is still in full effect.

Journal Page

Jennifer Smith

Dear Diary: Three Strikes Doesn't Mean You're Out

Who the hell came up with the term "dating," and why didn't anybody tell me it can be either the most complicated task on earth or the most revitalizing experience in life? The sad part is that I didn't learn this until the age of thirty! The frightening part is that I was learning all of this as a single mother while raising a teenage daughter. Sometimes life will hand you situations that not even the biggest glass of wine can ease. Uncork! Pour! Repeat! This is the story of my life. As a therapist, I'm sometimes criticized for not knowing better, but look—therapists are human too! If I could get a dollar for every time I heard "therapitize yourself," I could be rich, chilling somewhere on a Fiji island. But if that were the case, I wouldn't be talking to you right now.

My situation started when my husband cheated on me—and only went downhill from there! Back in high school, I never really had the chance to date. So when I got together with a charming man at age seventeen, it felt like a win. He was like chocolate, smooth and sweet . . . but bad for your teeth. I had his baby my junior year in college, and he proposed to me in the kitchen of our tiny apartment a mere four years later. We were together for eleven years and I felt on top of the world, getting ready to complete my master's degree—only to find that that fool had cheated on me.

After our divorce, I had to release him and move on. Some things just aren't fair, but as one good friend says, "What really is fair?" Today, those eleven years seem like a complete blur. I was disgusted with him, so it only makes sense that after the marriage ended, I wanted to have a little craziness, mixed with a little wild fun. I dated and it was fun! I needed to be free because I was still young and had needs. All women have them! Right?

Now, as a little girl from the Southside of Chicago, I was known for having a lot of thoughts going through my head. With all my crazy childhood experiences—from getting caught upside-down on the jungle gym with my undies showing in kindergarten to my sister never letting me live it down that I had traumatized her by crashing her into a wall playing choo-hoo train—my imagination has never been short of interesting. But my childhood exploits proved to be nothing compared to the things I would conjure up as an adult, especially when it came to dating.

Dating in the beginning was fun after the divorce. And it wasn't just sex (even though I am a Scorpio); I was finding my identity and discovering my own life lessons. I wanted to be reckless, since I missed that in my early twenties—but I began missing that true partnership that we're all destined to enjoy. Being wild feels great, but only until you realize that your bed is truly lonely at night. Additionally, you realize you have to be a role model for your daughter. You wise up for sure! I began to focus and look for something real. You know, that Adam and Eve biblical love! The together forever and secret haters wondering how you do it kind of love! Goofy, I know, but I still wanted it.

However, just because I was looking for something real and lasting didn't mean things were easy. In fact, it became the craziest baseball game of Can He Be the Next "One!" But in this game, three strikes does not mean you're out!

Let's start at the beginning. After getting rid of a few of my "fun boys," I met this quiet, smooth, charming chocolate brother. Lord knows I have a sweet tooth for that. I remember the night he walked me to my car even though it was raining. It was on and popping after that! I could tell that he would make a great father figure. He was everything I ever wanted, but there were two problems: first, my daughter hated him, and second, my attitude was an issue. After we had been together for a few years, all I could think was, "I'll be damned if this chocolate brother doesn't put a ring on it!" Why wouldn't he? We had been together three years and I loved him. Plus, we were not getting any younger! Everyone had a tendency to remind me of that, too. But eventually, the pressures of deciding what was best for me, him, and my daughter became too much. He wasn't ready and I needed to focus on finding someone for the future, not for "right now." It became my obsessive priority, because society tells you that something is wrong with you if you don't have a husband. We broke up. I did some soul searching and there was counseling all around.

A year or so later (along with a fat diamond ring on my sister's hand), I started the whole rollercoaster ride again. Here we go again; the pressures of "you need to get back out there!" became the chorus and constant song. Funny how people feel bad for you when they're happy—as if you aren't! Maybe being happy is a contagious spirit.

I guessed it was time to dust the cobwebs off, so I gave dating another try. I decided to take things up a notch and give a fair chance to everyone. After all, I'd heard often enough that we women have too high of standards and don't give the brothers a chance. Well, I gave it a chance . . . but never again! I ended up with a guy who had a few kids, smoked weed, and had massive anger issues. He was batshit crazy! After that was finished, I could only ask myself, "Girl, what were you thinking?"

After that fiasco, I turned up the heat with the scary little world known as "online dating." I told myself, why not? The result? Jesus take the wheel! Never mind . . . Just take the whole car! Nope . . . Just throw it all away! The internet will make you *lose your mind*, especially if you suck at discernment! But then, that's what your therapist is for.

After waiting a bit, I decided to try again. I had taken a year to grow as a person and to build up my business and further my career, and I was enjoying life with my daughter. I was in a position to meet someone new—yet secretly, I was back on my mission. This time, I wasn't trying so hard to find a father figure for my daughter, but I had the same desire for a partnership and to be able to model healthy partner relationships. I wanted to be married before forty!

After a few sour apples, I finally met a new guy that my daughter seemed to like a lot, and she loved his children as her own siblings. I thought I had achieved success. We made it all the way up to marriage counseling. Then everything crashed like an intense game of Jenga. Fears set in on his part and he started acting "dumb," as most women would say. I call it self-sabotaging. Funny how a man's past demons catch up with him when you add "Forever" and "Wife" to his daily repertoire. But by then, I had learned my lesson: Know your worth. You are not what society says you are. Single is not a curse. A man can only be ready on his own. And what would my daughter have to endure if things went bad like with her daddy? Divorce number two was not happening on my watch!

For me, the hardest part of dating after being divorced was being a model of healthy relationships to an adolescent girl. The next hardest part was letting go of people I loved when things didn't work out. I wanted my daughter to have a father figure in her life because we're told that men and fathers are important. It hurt to watch her struggle as she cycled through emotions. It was sad to watch her feelings of sadness turn into confusion, then to placing her father on a grandiose pedestal, and then to hatred because of his inability to be a presence in her life, all while dealing with my own struggles and fears. I wanted her to be like me, but at the same time, I wanted her not to be like me or to do the things I did.

While dating as a single mother, I learned that battling the many stereotypes about African-American women and relationships is hard. It becomes the social norm to be single and not feel worthy of successful love. But even though those relationships after my divorce did not end in forever, I thank those men for loving me as best they could, and I thank myself for allowing me to love again after my divorce. I learned a lot about brokenness in people, including myself.

My "first base" in the game of dating—he knows who he is—was magical, as he showed me that unconditional love is real, and I thank him for that. But the pressures of "why don't you have a ring yet" continued down the years of dating. Also, trying to date when your daughter is struggling is very difficult. It's hard to juggle what you want versus what she needs and to determine which decision is right. In the end, the stress of those two issues, along with underdeveloped identities for both of us, finished that relationship as we grew apart. I mourned that loss for a year, even though he was only a phone call away. But I can say today that we are still good friends.

I don't even know how I got to "second base;" it was a season of desperation. We all have had those moments. But I did learn that I can have standards and stick to them. I quickly ran to "third base," but learned that I didn't need to be married to be whole, to be happy, to raise my daughter, or to be a role model—and that still applies today. Looking back, I thought I was ready with my choices, but I wasn't. And that is okay. He was not ready. And that's okay too. We are good friends and I try to be a support for his children, even today. Sometimes I do regret the fact that I didn't provide my daughter with the two-parent household life I had growing up, or the Disney princess story we are so often lied to about, but that's okay, because our life is beautiful and it's our story to tell. It is unique in its own way. I challenge any single mother today: How is your story unique?

Dear Daughter:

What I want you, daughter, to learn from this phase in my life is that I tried my best, the best way I knew how! I apologize for my mistakes. It was hard, trying to keep from crying in front of you as I attempted to balance what you wanted, as well as your disappointment in not getting it, with my trying to get what I thought I wanted. I don't want you to hold grudges or get an attitude of bitterness toward all men from seeing my relationships, my tears, and my fears. How many times do we hold grudges toward things that don't even matter anymore in life? People are only human. Learn how to forgive and let go! Girls model what their role models do, and my fear was that you might end up in a similar situation. I want you to be able to take your time and choose wisely.

Make choices based off of what you want, not because of pressures caused by having a child early in life. Don't feel like you have to conform to American stereotypes. If you get married, make sure it is for the right reason, when God has brought you the right person with whom you want to enter that covenant, not just because your friends are doing it or because you want a ring, dress, and ceremony. Stay prayerful. The key to happiness is much more than whether you are in a relationship or not. Be careful that you don't turn "having a man" into an idolized concept. I know dating, sex, and friendships, and their effect on your identity, are really important for teenagers, but don't let that push you into something you don't want. Understand that oftentimes people are on different journeys, just like you are. Even though your father was not there to teach you to stand up for yourself, remember that you deserve the best, and expect to be treated that way.

You are an individual; know your worth and who you are. Don't be afraid to love, don't be afraid to forgive, and don't be afraid to make mistakes. Be patient in all things. Singlehood is a blessing and a means to growth. When one gift disappoints, there are many more gifts given in life. It's okay to have high standards and walk away from things that don't meet that standard. You have that choice to have a relationship with yourself. I have learned from my experiences that I am a strong person and I am awesome; my relationship with God brings that out from within me. Daughter, I hope that you're watching and listening as I aspire to achieve my dreams. I want so much more for you. I want better for you! Take your time to get to know yourself. Ask yourself: Who am I?

It wouldn't be right for the therapist in me not to remind you to be mindful and be present in the world. Every day is a journey, and I know you won't always get it right. Just remember, when things break up and fall apart, that people are not monsters. Sometimes people are hurt by their own circumstances and have lost their self-worth in the process. Everyone is a little broken, and some aren't self-aware enough to seek healing.

I love you and thank you for being there for me. I love you for being caring and concerned for me. You're in a beautiful space of teenagehood, where you can figure things out, grow in love, and flourish. So, my message to you, and to all the young ladies around the world reading this entry, is to continue to grow and learn every day. Nobody's perfect! I hope that I've made you proud, because I've definitely made myself proud. I feel peace in knowing that you can lead yourself to the last base in the game: Home! Where is home for you?

Journal Page

Kiana Shaw

....

Dear Diary: My First Love Was Not Lovely at All

Bradley Jackson was an academic achiever, a hard worker at a local pizza place, and a football player. He was so handsome to me. He had that bad boy swagger but that good boy reputation. He came from an affluent family so he always had and wore the latest and greatest. All of this helped his chances with the girls in our community because he had what they wanted... a car (it wasn't new but he was rollin'), money (girls tipped him well when he delivered their pizza—going so far as to ask for him by name), and visibility (being on the football team meant he had access to all of the parties).

I didn't care about all of that stuff though. I wasn't even allowed to date when I first met him, so his car and money meant nothing to me. I really just thought he was a cute guy, and the fact that he showed interest in me really made me feel special. I believed, at the time, he thought I was just as cute ... homely looking, but cute. It wasn't until later that I discovered that I was really just a conquest to him. See, as one of the few virgins in the youth group I participated in with his friends, I became a target to "take down." Yes, he grew to love me over time, because he got to know me and to understand the value my heart brought to his life, but that was an accident that came with investing time into me. He needed to work harder to get to access to me and to manipulate me into breaking rules, sneaking out, or sneaking him in. It was all the price he had to pay to have sex with me.

I loved the attention he gave me. I loved that he felt that I was worthy of him at a time when I didn't feel that way. Not only did I not feel worthy, I didn't feel pretty or beautiful or anything else for that matter, especially in comparison to some of the girls that were in my youth group. He wasn't a member of our program, but he would come around because he had a lot of friends that were in it, so he was able to participate sometimes when he didn't have sports or his job to go to. That allowed us to spend some time together even though we couldn't let it be known that we were a couple.

About a year and a half into our relationship he went away to military school. I was okay with that because he told me it was an all-boy school and he had nothing to do all day but think of me. Well, what I soon discovered was that next to that all-boy school ... was an all-girl school! He started seeing some college girl, and I was so hurt once I became aware of it. He wrote her off to me as a substitute—and then I found out he was engaged to some other lady, and a third lady was pregnant with his child and trying to decide if she should have an abortion or keep the baby. JESUS! See, back then, he was pretty predictable, and I figured out the password to his voicemail. I would call him and, once it went to voicemail, I would press * and then enter his password after the prompt. I found out ALL the goods. But I didn't leave, because he convinced me that it was a mistake, and that those women were just there because he missed me so much that he needed someone to fill the void so he wouldn't be so distracted. Yep! I fell for it.

See, I was just a girl who hadn't left Compton, dating the eighteen-year-old man who was traveling the country and going into the military. He was experiencing life, and I couldn't compete with college girls who didn't even have a curfew. Sex was the only way to stay in the competition for his heart. It wasn't even good sex, just "because this is what I am supposed to do with the man I love" sex. But even with that, I was still in another state and could only compete during spring and holiday breaks. I decided to send him nude photos to get him through the rough times . . . that didn't work.

He would come home and want to spend time with me, but we were splitting that time with his family and friends. I got what was left over, at night. And if it wasn't about sex, he was very aloof. I would confront him about it, crying, then we would make up and have make-up sex—and then it would start all over. I grew addicted to the drama of making him prove his love for me. I grew addicted to that feeling of *am I enough?* and the constant making up. I grew addicted to the adrenaline that came from him finally calling after leaving me hanging all day.

I grew to love that stuff, and it's really unfortunate, because I spent a lot of nights hurt, crying, and trying to understand why I wasn't worthy and how he could do this to me when I loved him so much. I spent a lot of nights wondering why he was cheating on me, why he wouldn't call me back, and why he would take me somewhere and give me roses one day and the very next day pull a disappearing act.

I still didn't leave him though. I had self-esteem issues. Sure, I could talk a good game, I could motivate other people, I could tell everybody else how great they were (not that I really ever truly saw how great they were—you can only see greatness in others after you can see it in yourself; I just knew the right things to say to people to make them feel good), but I never believed that I was great and worthy of more. We couldn't even have deep conversations, because he was limited outside of talk about the military and video games. So the only way to go beyond the surface was to ask "do you love me?" or "why are you cheating on me?" If it wasn't drama-filled, he would be aloof. On some level, I believe he became addicted to drama, too.

Our relationship lasted over four years, and in that time, I caught several sexually transmitted infections from him. At one point, the nurse at my doctor's office pulled me to the side and said, "Kiana, it is time to break up with him before you get something we can't cure." I was so mad at her about that, because her words stung the very core of me.

I kept going back because I based my value on what he thought of me. I allowed my value to be what he set it to. And if he didn't raise my value, then it was not raised. He was emotionally abusive and he knew that I always took the responsibility for whatever wasn't right in our relationship, so he kept making everything my fault.

The day I decided that I had had enough, he was pissed! I walked away, not caring anymore, not taking his calls; we couldn't block people back then so I just had to turn my ringer off. I was determined to put him behind me—and that is when he got crazy. That's when he started parking on the side street where he could watch my house and putting bouquets of roses on my porch at least twice a week. Once, he put his legs under my car to keep me from driving off. He would show up at my school with his gun on the seat next to him and tell me to get into his truck. When I would say no, he would threaten to harm everyone inside if I didn't leave with him—and I knew he was serious. I went with him one time because he was crying and I thought he was really hurting, but I spent the entire time in fear for my life. I had to tell him that my father was meeting me at the school for lunch just so he would take me back to school. I remember crying, knowing that he was trying to control me, but also knowing that he worked in law enforcement and carried his guns everywhere, so I had to be smart and cautious. But despite all that, I would not take him back. All of that, and he was still dating someone else!

I ended up filing a restraining order against him and I asked for my nude photos back. Of course he couldn't find them. He probably still has them. We broke the restraining order a few times because we did miss one another, but each time, he got more and more comfortable while I just wanted to go on with my life. I didn't want him anymore, or so I thought.

Years later, I saw someone close to him at a restaurant and she called him and brought me the phone. Hearing his voice brought back every single loving feeling and exciting twinge inside of me. I sure did miss him. Every inch of me got caught up in that moment and I agreed to let him have my number. I mean, we were adults now, right? That was years ago, right? It's in the past, right? So we met at a local mall and he was still handsome, still smelled good, and I still wanted him. He was extremely successful and seemed milder, calmer, and safer. He had grown up in our years apart.

After a few meetings, we started having sex, and eventually I got a call from him that was all too familiar. He told me he thought he had an STI and that I should go get checked.

WHAT? AS AN ADULT? ARE YOU KIDDING ME?! I told him not to ever contact me again, that I was not the scared little girl he used to know and that I had my own guns now. I hung up, thinking, "How the hell could I let this happen?"

I was talking to my dad one night after that and told him I ran into Bradley. Before I could go further, he said, "It's not fair to us for you to contact him, because we went through that relationship with you. We went through that breakup with you. We filed the restraining order with you. We went to court with you. And it is not fair if we have to kill him when you could just walk away from him." That conversation was what made me realize I had gone backward and that it was time to forgive myself and correct my course.

Dear Daughter:

I want you to understand that when you love yourself, you set a standard that everyone must meet. Men who want to be with you will rise to that standard; maintain it and they will raise it. I once read a quote that said "the moment you settle, you get less than what you settled for." Those words ring true like the gospel.

You are the prize! You should be worked hard for. You should be pursued. You should be treated as though you are the treasure a man has hunted for all of his life. Maintain your standard and walk away from anyone who says it is too high or unrealistic, because it isn't. They have just told you they don't see your value or your specialness.

Put the phone down. Stop calling him so much. He will never miss you if you "check in" with him every time you make a move. Stop tagging yourself to prove you were where you said you would be. Don't even post the photos until the next day. Let him think about you. Let him find you.

Men are hunters by nature. Women are the choosers. Women are the guiding force of society. We bring the morals and values needed to sustain our families, communities, and country. When we lose that specialness of our moral fiber by becoming "one of the guys," they stop needing and wanting to step up.

I was so busy trying to prove to him that I was the one he needed that I lost myself instead. You see, sweetie, our emotions and hormones lead us when we let them loose for the first time, because we have never had the experience of dealing with them before. They take over our minds and bodies. It's like we're possessed. Our bodies are feelings new things and we mistake that newness for love. We get addicted to that sensation. The truth of it all is that while our bodies are saying yes to sex, our emotions don't know how to say no to it. As we move forward in relationships, we don't necessarily learn how to navigate this uncharted territory, and the people in our lives are usually so embarrassed by their own journey that they don't tell us the downside to love. No one really tells us that we're more curious than we are ready, and because of that, we go in with all this curiosity, ready to give our bodies, give our hearts, give our emotions, give our love to some individual with absolutely no requirements from him, because we don't know to have requirements yet.

Listen, you are more than your breasts and vagina. You are more than a conquest. You must spend time learning yourself and understanding who God says you are, so that no one else can assign you an identity. Go to dinner and the movies alone. Travel the world with your friends, and sometimes, go places by yourself and meet people when you get there.

If I would have known then what I know now, I would have waited until I got married to have sex. Eighteen- to twenty-five-year-old guys don't know how to value a woman. They aren't ready to meet your standards; shoot, they don't even know they are supposed to set any themselves.

Learn from my mistakes and then go conquer your world.

Journal Page

Mara Monique

Dear Diary: Being Grown Doesn't Come from Age

I've always liked being with older people, so it made sense when I married a man who was eight years older than me. What didn't make sense was how he would often remind me of my age, since to him it meant I wasn't as mature as he was. I believed him. At that time, I was twenty-eight years old, married, and a mother of four children, yet I was still struggling to feel "grown." I looked forward to getting out of my twenties, as I thought that at that point I would indeed be "grown" and would finally be treated as such by my husband.

I struggled to get my husband's attention and affection after the first year we were together. I should have realized he was not the man for me, but if there is one thing I am known for, it is my stubbornness. I tried all the things that I heard everyone talk about—things like prayer, therapy, showing my anger, getting a makeover, kindness, and more—to save my marriage. Nothing seemed to help. All it did was make it more obvious that the man I married didn't want me or love me any longer. I was overcome with the hurt and shame of not being loved by my husband, as well as the fear of raising four children alone, so I silently stayed in the marriage.

My husband had convinced me that being under thirty meant I was immature. That created my new answer to saving my marriage: make it to thirty without a divorce. If I could make it in the marriage until I turned thirty, my husband would finally, miraculously love me as a grown woman. My thirtieth birthday finally freed me of my twenties and made me, I thought, officially grown! But as I stood looking out of the window over my kitchen sink, I realized I felt the same as I did the week before. I was confused. Does this mean I'm still not grown? I asked myself. Maybe this is just who I am, immature.

I knew my husband would never want me as an immature woman. I was too silly and clumsy, which always bothered him. I smiled and laughed too much, according to what he told me. Often I played silly games with my kids that created messes. Sometimes we would all end up rolling around the living room floor having fun, only to turn and see him with a look of displeasure over my actions. It was clear that I wasn't the wife he wanted me to be. I was a young, fun-loving mother. My children loved me being their fun-loving mommy, and

I loved being her. I figured that it was decided, five to one, and I would stay fun loving. All I had to do was convince my anti-fun husband that being fun loving was not irresponsible, that it was possible to smile, play, and laugh a lot while still being responsible. Once I accomplished that, I thought, then I would be happy.

Two years later I was in the same space. I continued to try to impress him with my skill at mothering his children. I was raised believing that a husband loves his wife for being a good mother to their children. It was instinctual to take great care of the children and the home in general. In his opinion, though, I often fell short when it came to dinner time and keeping an immaculate house. Even though I worked outside of the home and maintained 90 percent of the responsibility for the children's care, I believed him. I could do better. I color coded almost everything pertaining to the kids to simplify organization for everyone. It worked well, except it seemed my husband refused to go by the color coding. It would cause turmoil at times, since we all were used to the color coding. It made me think he loved disrupting the household system.

He didn't do negative things like stay out running the streets all night and not making it home; I was grateful for that. But although he stayed home at night, he also kept to himself, no matter how hard I tried to engage with him. I had lost myself in trying to be what he liked. I knew I was losing him, I just didn't realize I was losing me as well.

Then my mother was diagnosed with Stage 4 cancer; it was terminal. I became deeply depressed. The truth of my life was that if I wasn't depending on my husband, then I was obeying my mother, as she orchestrated my life as well. I knew I was being controlled, but it was normal for me. Now my life curator was dying. I felt rebellious and ready to leave all my safety nets. Since death was coming, I was going to throw divorce in too. But my beautiful, wise mother had one more directive for me before she ascended. A deathbed promise like you see on television, except she wasn't asking. She told me she wouldn't worry about my kids and me as long as I didn't divorce my husband. I had tears in my eyes when I told her I felt my husband didn't even like me. "Doesn't matter, he provides well, and I know he will take care of you and those babies. It brings me peace knowing y'all will be okay after I'm gone," my mother insisted. She passed on a short while later. I was obedient. I stayed with him.

There I was, shackled by a dying wish from my first, most beloved jailer, my mother. I was dying inside. My children needed a happy mommy, but by that point she only popped in for brief appearances. Fortunately, the Lord sent me a way to raise my spirit through my amazing mother-in-law, who directed me to the Bible. Prayer eased my pain and supported my journey out of depression. Although my circumstances in my home had not changed, I focused differently. I became very active with my children's sports. My jailer/husband, to whom my mother gave her puppeteering rights upon her death, didn't appreciate my attention being on things outside of the house. In other words, he felt I shouldn't be coaching youth sports if I couldn't keep up my wifely and motherly duties. Rather than fight, I just tried to make it all work. I did pretty good. We can really amaze ourselves at times when we want something to work out.

I must not have been doing as well as I thought, though. I had been faking it for so long I ignored the effects of the truth. I secretly cried, often. My mother-in-law was the only one that loved my husband more than I did, so I confided in her. I didn't want to hear anyone trash him, as I figured my friends and family would if they heard my side. She was encouraging to me. She knew I didn't spend much money on myself, so she would send me money and insist I spend every penny on myself. Also, she told me I "bet' not" tell her son. She also explained that I shouldn't tell him everything anyway. My mother had told me that, but it didn't sound as devious coming from his mother. I decided it must be right, so that's what I did.

One day I ran into a childhood friend. He was quite flirtatious. It made me smile, even though I knew it was wrong. He complimented me, but I felt it wasn't genuine. I told myself he just wanted something sexual from me. Too bad, so sad, I thought to myself, I'm a married woman and I don't cheat. However, I decided that just talking from time to time was okay. He sure made me laugh. Nothing wrong with having a funny and nice friend. His humor was a breath of fresh air compared to my stoic, anti-fun husband, who didn't talk to me much anyway. My husband barely noticed my existence—until I began smiling too much. He knew he wasn't the cause, and that he had to do something.

My husband bought our family a six-bedroom, five-bathroom house as an attempt to make things better with our marriage. I admit, I was the one that wanted the house and he provided it. Like my mom said, he was a good provider. I thought that maybe it didn't matter if he loved me as long as he was a good provider. Maybe it didn't matter that my name wasn't on the mortgage or deed of the new house, as he tried to convince me. It definitely was an interesting fact though. I sweetly asked, how is it "ours" if only your name is on it? On cue I was met with hostility for having a question about finance-related subjects. Hostile reactions became the norm for me. I left it alone. I decided that maybe it didn't matter, since California is a community property state and we were legally married. No reason to have another battle while we were trying to mend our relationship.

I had no official bills to pay. I was free to spend my money on what I wanted. But my mommy guilt had me spending every dime on my beautiful new house and my children. I tried to save, but most months my husband wanted some electronic toy that he couldn't necessarily afford, since he paid all the bills. I was always more than happy to give him the money, hoping he would be happy with me. He wasn't. He came to expect it. He was no longer the provider he used to be. I thought, if only my mother could see him now. I wonder if she would hold me to my promise?

The Lord blessed us with that newly built, huge, beautiful house. We were able to choose everything in it from the ground up. From the outside looking in, it would seem I had an amazing life. I had dreamed about a home like that one when I was younger. I first learned that dream was possible when my aunt and uncle had their home built in Texas when I was a child. I didn't know how I was going to get it, I just knew I wanted it. Thank God my lack of knowledge didn't stop the possibility from reaching me, I thought as I walked around my personal model home. It was so big, sometimes I would forget about a couple rooms that we didn't use much.

It didn't take long for my dream home to become my house of horrors, however. I felt like a stranger in the house I chose. The décor I coordinated began to seem foreign to me. The house was so large, but that made it easier to hide in plain sight. The children spent their days and nights in their game room. The game room was the best distraction for all of them, as it gave me more time to not have to pretend I was fine. I still had five more bedrooms and a den to hide in to wallow in my sorrow.

My misery was apparent; I had good reason. I would ask myself, How long can I survive this life? How can I admit to the world my husband doesn't want me? Even worse, I had found out he wanted another man's wife. He had gotten involved with a woman whose actions did not fit the wife and mother standards he expected of me. I was so confused. He had always expected me to act like a proper wife and mother. This woman did not fit the description he gave me. Everything was a lie! My whole existence with this man was a falsehood. Now that I could see it clearly, what was I going to do? He maintained control of all the household finances. I had no clue about any of it, just as he wanted. It became clear for the first time that he was truly happy. He had me, the babysitter/housekeeper, while he had another man's wife to run off and play with at his leisure. I was hopeless and ashamed about my reality. My husband was so arrogant. When he would lie about where he was going he would smirk. My heart hardened inside while I raged on the outside. He wasn't moved. He had things his way.

One morning he showed me the power he felt he had over me. Smiling as he walked to where I was sitting, he dropped some mail in front of me. It was a letter from Cottonwood Place Apartments, addressed to me, but it was already opened. I pulled the paper out and read it. It said there was a three-bedroom apartment available that they were offering me if I was still interested. Back when my mom was still alive, I had felt some rare strength, so I had applied to move into a low-income apartment with a plan to leave him. They had put me on the waiting list over a year ago. Reading the letter gave my heart hope. According to the letter I had to contact them by—as my eyes filled with water—last week. Then I understood why he was smiling; he knew that this opportunity for me to move out of his house had passed. Why would he block it? Didn't he want the chance to be with his mistress and let me go? Instead he chose to open my mail and keep my escape from me. As I sat there, crying as quietly as possible, it was evident I was where he planned to keep me. I silently died inside.

I turned to my Bible. It directed me back to his mother. I was hoping my mother-in-law could help me find a way to be okay with my marriage and to accept her cheating, lying, cruel son so I could keep my mother's dying wish. To my surprise, she was upset and cried with me. She told me she didn't care what date was on that letter, I better call them first thing in the morning and beg. If that didn't work, she told me to go down there to beg and cry in person. I couldn't believe my ears. Was she telling me to leave her son? Was she telling me to fight for myself? I felt supported for the first time, like my feelings mattered and I needed to put them first. I felt empowered. I made that call. The kids and I moved in a few weeks later—without his prior knowledge. He wasn't the only one who could keep a secret.

Making the move was terrifying. I couldn't let my fear deter me, though, because through it all I had my children to consider. I wanted to get my mind right while trying not to disrupt their lives too much. Easier said than done. It wouldn't matter what I did, their lives were disrupted in multiple ways. I could only make it as comfortable a space as possible. To do that, I had to leave life with their father. I reassured them that he would still very much be in their lives. It seemed they believed me.

My soon-to-be-ex-husband started talking to me more than ever before, begging or belittling me for hours on the phone. My goal was to be nice enough that he wouldn't abandon my children and would pay me some sort of child support. I was fearful of going to get court-ordered child support, because he made me believe that it would jeopardize his employment, since he worked for the California Superior Courts. It didn't matter much that I had moved out of his house, he still controlled me in many ways. The fact I still loved him was also a huge factor. I still wanted him to at least like me. I allowed him to control the amount of money he felt I deserved to care for his children. That amount would fluctuate depending on my behavior. He also decided he would have the children on weekends, every weekend. I asked for at least one weekend and he flipped out. I let it go.

His arrangement gave me no choice except to grin and bear it or suffer his passive-aggressive withholding of child support. Eventually I found the strength to go to the courts. I mentally prepared to have someone working at the courthouse look at me as his evil wife that they had heard stories about. The reality was very different. The place was huge—and a completely different building than he worked in. My imagined fear bubbles began popping one by one. I stayed calm and honest during the proceedings and the court awarded me seven times what he would sometimes give me. Some of my self-doubt left. I was grown now, right?

Even though we were eventually divorced, it wouldn't be until years later that I truly broke free of his mind manipulations. Being grown meant that, when I was tired of being sick and tired, I took full control of my life. I finally knew I didn't need any man. I didn't even want one. Yet my doubts seemed to linger around me whenever I dated. Why? Was I that great? It seemed the answer was yes. Great in a sense of being an open soul to their needs, while I easily slipped back into the self-sacrificing behaviors of my past. That only led to heartache and pain. The cycle needed to end. I heard of a new term, self-love, on a TV show. People who considered themselves self-loving appeared happier than I had ever been. I decided I needed to find out how to become self-loving.

To love myself I needed to get to know myself. It was interesting learning about myself. I've been what seems like multiple people throughout my lifetime. I really needed to know who I was. I felt lost when there weren't any outside forces causing me discomfort—clearly a sign of a confused mind. Not, as I learned, how a self-loving person would behave. A person who exhibits self-love is honest with themselves first, and that enables them to choose options that reflect their self-worth.

I began to speak up for myself. It felt great. I didn't worry about the reaction I would get. There wasn't any malicious intent behind the things I said. Besides, I can't control anyone's reaction except my own. These mantras were on repeat in my head. My learned behavior of forsaking myself for others had to end. People began treating me differently. I used to be quiet with my input, just conceding to whatever came up; instead, I began to interject. At times, I had to channel various female music artists to find strength. Their song lyrics became my therapy. Powerful words sung by powerful women helped to empower me. They spoke on the possibilities that I couldn't see. It helped keep self-doubting thoughts out of my mind. I believed it and made it become my truth. It is my faith in the greatness Jehovah has given all of us that keeps me inspired and moving forward.

Dear Daughters:

Remember, you have an amazing spirit; protect it. I believe this is the key, and I wish I had known it sooner. I would have protected my spirit better and been able to mother you better. Protecting your spirit doesn't mean building a wall and shutting off relationships. The protection you need is the opposite. You need to keep your mind open to love. It is easier said than done, but it is 100 percent possible. Protect your spirit by getting to know yourself better and falling in love with yourself. This will make you more honest with yourself. Once you get in the habit of being honest with yourself, you will undoubtedly make better choices for yourself.

Another benefit from truly loving yourself is that you become more empathic. Loving and respecting yourself allows you to get out of your own way and see things from another's point of view. This will cause you to act with compassion. You will gain discernment, which helps with lessening stress about things you cannot control while letting you know what you can control. This allows you to know that you are still a good person, even when you answer "no" to someone or when your lack of compliance may rub someone the wrong way. Please realize wholeheartedly that you cannot control anyone's emotions or actions, only your own. Know that for certain and live by it. Refuse to do anything that may cause you pain. Know that you are smarter and stronger mentally than you may give yourself credit for. Know your worth. Learn that life always goes on, and so should you. I love you more than air and will always be here for you. You are amazing!

Journal Page

Tasha Champion

Dear Diary: When You're Racing Yourself, You're Going to Lose

I am incredibly grateful for where I am today. I no longer do the chase for love I did year after year. My feet are no longer tired and my heart no longer breaks from running after love and acceptance. It was only when I began to love myself that I could stop chasing after it.

The smile I wear today, the happiness I feel, the joy I have, they're so authentic—but boy did it take time to get here. The tears, the pain, the hurt, the drama: it was always something when I was running after love. I can probably trace it back to being a little girl and simply feeling unsupported. The things I wanted to do, to act, sing, and dance, were not supported. I was a cheerleader and no one ever came to my games. I was taunted for being an emotional child. In middle school I was teased to no end because of the things I didn't have. Over the years, all those feelings began to settle in me as if I were nothing more than this person who no one supported, this person who everyone teased. I didn't grow up with "I love you" being said around the house; it was assumed that we just knew. I felt that the love I saw others have was disrupted and disconnected from me. That began a journey of chasing a feeling I have wanted to have since I was a child, to simply be supported, accepted, and loved for being me. Not knowing how to find it within myself, I looked for others to provide it. For sixteen years, I accepted unacceptable behavior from people. I ran after unhealthy relationships and practically begged for those people to see something in me worth loving.

I became the track star runner who wasn't running after the gold medal. I was nineteen when I found myself pregnant by a guy named Reed who I had been dating for about three months. I met him at the school we were both attending. Although he was a pretty nice guy, I wasn't ready to have a baby so early on. Once he revealed my pregnancy to his family, they were completely against it, going so far as to blame me for getting pregnant, telling him it was my problem and strongly encouraging me to have an abortion, which was an absolute NO. Then, to put the icing on the cake, toward the end of my pregnancy I found out he was still sleeping with his ex—I was the rebound girl to their breakup. Thinking I had the edge over her since I was pregnant, I laced up my shoes to start my race. I was going to show him that I was so much better for him; after all, we were having a baby and he was living with me. I confronted him and, like with all men, I heard everything from *I'll stop talking to her* to *I want to be here with you and the baby*.

I made the decision to believe him, only to find, by the time my daughter was a year old, that he was back talking to his ex. That started the back and forth, he's with me, he's with her, he's back with me, then with her . . . then, all of a sudden, there was no more her. Guess what, I WON! But not really, because she was instantly replaced by another woman, and another, one after the other. Every time he would say that things weren't working for him, I fought to keep us together. I couldn't bear to feel the aftermath of him being gone—even though all along I was feeling that same thing with him there. It got to the point where if he said he was running to the store, I was 95 percent sure I wouldn't see him for hours or even until the next day. The back and forth went on for seven years, with us having two more kids during that time.

This abnormal behavior had become my normal. He had been telling me for years that I wasn't the one and that he didn't care what I did, yet I still chased after him because I needed to show him I *was* the one. But one day, all of a sudden, that message clicked. Since he didn't care what I did, I decided to do what I wanted. While on a trip out of state to visit family, I met up with a childhood friend. We had liked each other as kids, but as adults it was different. We had a great time. I let the night happen and it was well worth it.

Within two weeks of my return home, Reed had found out about me having sex with someone else. He said he didn't care, yet I received a plethora of name calling. Needless to say, it was the end. He left and, for the first time, I didn't run after him. It took me seven years to get to that point—and in seven days he returned and asked me to marry him. In my mind, again, I WON! All of the fussing, fighting, not giving up, telling him how much being with me was best for him, attempting to prove I was better than the next—and now he wanted to marry me. I was at the finish line, drained and exhausted, but the gold medal was in my hand.

I honestly didn't believe in the marriage, but I certainly convinced myself that I could. I mean, after all, he had said he would only marry once, and hell, I was the one he asked. As I walked down the aisle, I could hear God tell me, don't do it. I gave God the hand and told him I got this, and nothing was stopping me. Really, all I wanted was to show people, especially his family, that I won; we were getting married despite all of their negative thoughts and comments. BIG MISTAKE!

Within the first three months, there were already other women. There I was, lacing up my shoes again. Why not? I was his wife; we had a family. I was absolutely convinced that this man, who I know never loved me, could love me, and I was willing to run the distance. We had another child and I ran us to another state. I thought that with a new move, a fresh start, we should be good. I could get him away from people he had cheated on me with and he would focus on me. Internally, though, I was screaming for a divorce. My daughter, who was twelve at the time, looked at me and said, "I love him, but why don't you just divorce him?" I didn't have an answer, because deep inside I knew she was right. I kept thinking if I could just do this, just do that, get him to do this, get him to do that, then I could feel loved and be loved. Was that too much to ask for? I thought I could love him enough that he would eventually love me, and that the idea of family that I had built in my mind would become our reality.

We moved and nothing changed. Why would it? I was traveling between two states, working, paying all the bills, and giving him sex when he wanted; and although I was in pain on the inside, I stayed smiling on the outside. I would come home to find his phone full of messages and explicit pictures from other women.

I began to spend as much time away as I could. I started hanging out and reconnected with an old high school crush; although it wasn't going to develop into anything, it was a welcome distraction, because I felt wanted. The more I was away from Reed, the more I started looking at him with exasperation. I'd been dealing with him for more than ten years; what the hell was I expecting to change? I wanted it to work, but I also wanted the strength to leave . . . and then in walked Jan, a sergeant in the military.

We became friends a few months after we met. It began as an honest friendship. We shared common interests and we were both seeking for love, and eventually she and I would find what we thought was love within each other. We began a whirlwind affair, always wanting to be with each other. It was easy to be with her because I wanted to be away from him so badly. She was the only person I told that I wanted a divorce, but that I was afraid of my children hurting.

Finally, after a message I heard at church—a message where the pastor said "some of y'all are married to people you have no business being married to"—I made the decision. I told Reed it was time for a divorce. He said he didn't care and that he knew about my affair with Jan. Of course he knew; he would go through my phone, and I'm not one to delete anything. I wasn't even hiding the affair. I honestly didn't care, because I was done. The thought of my marriage turned my stomach. What happened next, though, no one could have ever prepared me for: Reed said that when he left, he would be leaving everything behind; he didn't even want to be a father anymore. The next morning he sat our children down and told them that we were getting a divorce and he would no longer be their father, explaining that he needed to restart his life as if he was never married and had never had children. His voice was shaky and his eyes watered while I silently dared him to drop a tear. Even now, in 2018, my children have not heard from their father again.

I immediately jumped into a relationship with Jan and we both thought it was something real. It was easy to feel like that. She wanted a family, and I had one. I wanted to be loved, and she wanted someone to love. She helped me a lot when I had pretty much lost everything, including over half my income. The first year was great—but looking back, that's because she was deployed. The following two years were hell. Anything she had done or did for me, she threw in my face. She was a raging bully toward my children and eventually became a bully toward me. I was so engulfed in trying to be loved that I did not protect my children the way I should have. Through all of it, I was again trying to show her why she should love me, trying to hold on to something unhealthy, a false sense of love. I was repeating the chase. I wanted her to love me; I wanted to connect with her the way I never could with my husband. The more I pushed for us, the more it became clear that it would never be.

Finally it hit me: I needed her to love me the same way I needed my husband to love me because *I* wasn't loving me. All that I was giving to everyone else, I wasn't giving to myself. I was surrounded by people and I felt so alone. I was laughing on the outside and drowning in my tears on the inside. What was I teaching my children? Something had to change. When I felt God tell me it was time for me to love me, I listened. I ignored him on my wedding day, and I was not about to do it again.

I decided to go on a spiritual journey of self-love and discovery. I could not spend another year running after someone to love me. It was time that I learned the depth of loving myself. This is where life completely changed for me. In loving myself, I found love in its purest and most authentic form. All that I was searching for in others was within me. I spent a year learning the tools and lessons I needed and another year applying them. I am forever grateful that God hadn't given up on me. He showed me my strength and power and, more importantly, the love that lives in me—and no one can ever take that from me, nor will I ever give it away.

Dear Daughter:

You are more powerful than you may know. To know your power is to always stand in your truth with love and compassion.

There is no one more important in your world than you. Love yourself first, because you come first. This is not selfish; it is selfless. You will give and receive love in the most genuine ways when it comes from within. I encourage you to use my experience and my truth as lessons learned and not as lessons repeated. I watched my mom fight for a marriage that wasn't good for her and I repeated what she did. You get to break that chain. You get to know your value and worth much earlier than I did. When you look in the mirror, know the person that is looking back at you. Love her, for she is incredible, unstoppable, intelligent, and beautiful, with a kind heart, a caring soul, and a wonderful spirit. A lot will come your way, some good, some not so good; either way, be ready to learn the lesson and it will let you grow. If you don't learn the lesson, it will continue to appear in your life until you do. Attach yourself to the God that's in you. He will give you the life you dream of and desire when you follow what he puts into your spirit. When you know, love, and see yourself the way God knows, loves, and sees you, no one will ever be able to force on you an identity you didn't create for yourself.

Be bold and brave enough to step outside your comfort zone. I couldn't do that for myself; I feared what was waiting for me on the other side. God removed all of my comfort and forced me to look at myself. What I found was a life worth living. Become the track star of your life; chase your dreams and goals and the success you want to reach. I ran in the wrong direction, and while I live with no regrets because it made me the woman I am today, I can only imagine the opportunities that would have been presented had I run toward my desires. Thank you for choosing YOU. Thank you for learning from the experiences I have shared with you and for commanding more out of your life. I know your journey will be different and you will experience your own storms and mountains to climb; just always remember that storms clear and you have the power to move mountains. Trust what God continues to give and show you, and you will never chase love, because you will know he has already instilled it in you. You owe it to yourself and the next generation of daughters to be your greatest self.

Journal Page

Tiffany Adams

Dear Diary: My Brother Was My Personal Angel

I lost my brother to brain cancer when I was just twelve years old, and it took a toll on me. His name was Larry, but everyone called him Fellas. Even though he was eleven months younger than me, he was my protector from all things. When I couldn't sleep because of night terrors, I used to run into his room and he would comfort me, telling me that everything would be okay. When I would look into his eyes I felt protected, because my brother was close to me and he made everything feel all right. I could go back to sleep when I was with him because instead of fear, I felt a sense of comfort.

When we were still young, my family moved to the tenth floor of the projects on the Southside of Chicago. It felt like we became part of a community of family members. Even though we were in a low-income building, everyone looked out for each other and watched over one another's children to make sure we could all have fun without leaving the building—and that allowed us to play on multiple floors and have even more fun. During the summers, our community provided breakfast, lunch, and snacks for all of the children. My mom made extra money on the side by selling icee cups. As I adjusted to living in the building, I even made some new friends.

My friend Ishea had a really mean cousin named Lisa who used to tag along with us. I went out of my way to be nice to Lisa, even running to the store in the morning before school to buy her candy. I did that for months—until the day she accused me of stealing from her. She said she gave me sixty cents for candy and I only gave her forty cents' worth of candy back. She actually wanted to fight me over it, but Ishea was there and she used her influence with the both of us to calm the situation. I thought the issues we had were over, but I was wrong. Lisa approached me while I was playing with Fellas and some of his friends in the hall. She wanted to start something. Lisa and I started to argue over the candy situation again and she pushed me. A tear fell down my face, and before I knew it, Lisa's head was going back and forth—but I didn't remember hitting her. That's when I realized it wasn't me! Fellas was beating her up. I stood there paralyzed, because I used to fight Fellas all the time and he never hit me. Instead, he would just cry. So I didn't even know he had it in him. I was shocked at his behavior, even though I understood that it was his way of protecting me; he was my personal angel who made sure that I was safe.

Fellas would also comfort me when our dad would yell at me for not understanding my math concepts. He didn't know how to say Tiffany when we were little kids, so he would say "Tenee, it's going to be okay." He would stick up for me and make sure I felt loved, and it made me feel like someone was right by my side, protecting me, at all times.

Fellas used to get seizures often, and we made frequent trips to the hospital, until one day my mother refused to leave until they could tell her why it was happening. That was the day they found an inoperable tumor on his brain. Chemotherapy would prolong his life, but it wouldn't save him; it would decrease the quality of his life and just be a temporary solution to extend our time with him. My parents agreed to the chemo, but Fellas slowly got worse. Fellas lost his eyesight, he lost his ability to walk without using his walker, and eventually he had no choice but to go to a wheelchair; he lost control of his hands, and finally he began to lose his appetite, which was when everyone realized that Fellas was going downhill and time was running out.

The hospital set Fellas up with a foundation that grants terminally ill patients their final wishes. When he was asked what he wanted, my brother told them he wanted them to buy Barbie dolls for me and my sister. While the lady from the foundation agreed to get me and my sister some dolls, she asked him to focus on something he would like. He thought for a moment and then said he wanted to go to Disney World—and they actually sent us there! The foundation went all out, paying for airline tickets for us all and making sure the fridge was stocked with our favorite foods. We even had full time transportation for our family, a private pool, a boat to go fishing in, and access to all of the theme parks. That was the most memorable moment that we had as a family; our family stopped thinking about Fellas' sickness and we just focused on having fun with each other.

Even as his body started to shut down, my best friend and protector was still looking out for me. One day, I got into trouble, and my dad told me I was getting a whooping. Fellas said, "I'll take Tenne's whooping for her, dad." My dad, as mean as he was, knew that he could not whoop Fellas, so he looked at me with slight compassion and said, "you get a pass this time." I remember being so grateful that my brother was still looking out for me; even when he was taking his last breath I still felt my protector was there, still watching over me.

After Fellas died, everyone in my family started doing their own thing. Years of abuse had built up resentment, and I was on a new road in a new world, which didn't include having protection or love in it. I went looking for love to replace what I lost in my brother's death, love that I should have gotten from my parents. I began to go through men like water, hoping to fill the void left by my brother's death. No one showed me how to mourn my brother or how to deal with his death, so I started acting out of character and began making bad choices. I didn't know what the love of a man was supposed to feel like, but I did know the depth of the love that my brother had had for me. I based my expectations of how men are supposed to treat me on the love I had from my brother, and I knew that I wouldn't settle for anything less than what I deserve.

I began looking for true love to replace the love from my brother, but the search did not end well; I was still dissatisfied. Instead, I taught myself how to play the game of love and sex and I learned to have my own agenda when going into relationships. If they didn't have a car or money, I would walk right off, just keep going my separate way, because I did not find what I was looking for. I learned that if I couldn't find the love I wanted, I would just use men for personal pleasure and personal gain when they did not meet my standards. I taught myself how to deal with the pain of losing my brother—but that consisted of me talking to any and every guy who would give me attention. I just wanted to ease the pain and get over the devastation of losing my brother, so I used sex to fill the void.

I discovered at the age of sixteen that I had cysts on my right and left ovaries. The doctors wanted to remove both of my ovaries and told me that once they did, I would never be able to have children. I begged my parents to have them just remove one of my ovaries because I really wanted to be a mom, but the doctor informed me that they needed to remove both, and that I would need to be on birth control for the rest of my life in order to keep the cysts from growing back. That kind of threw me into a new pattern of trying to numb the pain. Sex alone was not filling the void I felt after hearing I would not be able to have children, and I was still getting over the loss of my brother. I became very overwhelmed. So I started smoking weed, and eventually, I couldn't even go to sleep without first being high. But then I had somewhat of a spiritual awaking from God; I couldn't talk or move as he ministered to me about my life. It opened my eyes to see that the life I was living was not pleasing in God's eyes.

I really did want to be healed, but my parents' constant arguing made me need something outside of God for my healing. So I kept having sex and switched from weed to excessive drinking. I was still looking to things outside of God to fill the void in me. Then I met Randy and thought I had found God in a human form! We started going out after work, which meant I didn't have to hear the arguing and fighting that was going on in my home. The beginning of our relationship was amazing. Randy took me out and spoiled me all the time. I was finally happy. We opened up to one another; I shared the pain I had over the loss of my brother and he opened up to me about his family and how his parents also would fight and argue. Our stories became our common bond and connection with one another and we felt safe with one another.

I moved in with Randy after only knowing him for a few months—and discovered that this fairytale would not have a happily ever after. I went from sleeping in a bed to sleeping on the floor—but sometimes you have to deal with such things when you are in love. Then I went from three meals a day to one meal a day—and I was not bothered, because I still believed that it was true love, and that allowed me to keep pushing through. But then Randy started to be very violent toward me. He would make demands, and if I didn't say or do what he wanted me to, he would start hitting me. I remember him beating me so badly that I couldn't walk once he was done, so I had to drag myself across the floor to the bathroom. Of course, with each incident, he would profess his love and shower me with gifts and apologies. Every time he apologized I easily forgave him, because I wanted to hold on to the fairytale, even though deep down I knew it was not true.

I eventually grew tired of fighting him. The first time I decided to leave, Randy got a knife and grabbed me by the neck so hard I actually felt like I was going to die. I heard him yelling as he stabbed me in the back—but even then, I forgave him. I became pregnant with my oldest daughter and the fighting continued until she was three years old. That was when I decided I would die or live on my own terms. I told him that I loved our baby too much to allow her to be in the same situation that we both experienced growing up. It wasn't easy, but we tried to co-parent after that. For a while, he would come to my home to watch her on the weekends while I worked, but eventually even that stopped and I became a single mom.

I came to realize that life is not what it seems; there are no perfect fairy tales, as everyone experiences bumps and bruises, but you should never give up, because there are greater things in store for everyone. I have experienced good days and bad days, and I eventually realized that it's always important to remain who you are and to never settle for less than what you are.

I remember a time shortly after my brother's death when I was walking to my mother's room to go get something. I heard the trees hitting our window, and I heard my brother calling my name. I could not believe it at first—it did not feel real—but that was his way of letting me know that my personal angel and protector would always watch over me; even though I cannot see him, he is still around me and his eyes are watching over me. Knowing my brother is still watching over me gives me peace of mind, and I feel at ease because he will always be with me.

While it took me a long time to come to terms with my brother's death, in the end I realized that he is still watching over me. I know that my personal angel would want me to live the best life I can. I now strive to remember that pleasure only lasts for a moment, and that life and living well is more important. Everyone deserves to soar like an eagle.

Dear Daughter:

Never settle for less than what you are. I often share my mistakes with you to help you avoid making the same decisions that I made. I want you to take a different path than the one I did. I want your path to lead to success. I want you to succeed and not fail; I want to see you float and not sink; I want you to grow your wings and soar like an eagle. The world is in your hands, and the sky's the limit; you can do whatever you put your mind to.

I would have done a lot of things differently if I had had the proper wisdom and guidance, especially right after my brother died. I would have loved myself and stayed in school. I would have pursued education the way I pursued men, I would have chased my education and made men wait, because the more educated you are, the better the variety of men you can choose from, and you cannot live a good life without an education. Men are always going to be here, so make sure you have your life in order and make sure that you are happy with yourself. You want to be successful and prosper, not struggle. I also would have spent more time traveling the world and learning to stand on my own two feet, so that no one would stomp me with theirs. I would have been more independent, instead of relying on men for my happiness.

Daughter, never settle for less than who you are, because beauty lies both inside yourself and out. You're smart, so go to school and do not repeat the mistakes I made in my life because of my grief. I know you are smart and you have the world at your fingertips, so always remember to shoot for the stars; the sky's the limit.

Journal Page

Yolanda Allen

Dear Diary: Sometimes You Have to Grow Through What You Go Through

The standards or rules we live by are initially decided for us by our parents. As we age, this group of influencers grows to include others, such as family, community members, friends, and peers. Ultimately, though, each of us has to decide for ourselves what our standards are and why they matter. Extending respect to others and being treated with respect is important to me; it's a vital personal standard that became a part of my life during my first year of high school.

My mom, Margo, gave me a piece of advice on the heels of a breakup during my freshman year of high school: "If you allow a man to come in and out of your life, he'll never respect you." The personal power I gained from implementing her advice then had a transformative impact on my decision making in other situations involving respect through the years. I ended up making specific life decisions dealing with love, friendship, and marriage that were all influenced by this piece of advice.

That breakup was no ordinary high school breakup; it was a major event! We were a popular couple and had been together for over a year, for part of middle school and the beginning of high school, which is a very long time during the adolescent years. Oddly enough, we were a well-known couple despite being "scrubs." The morning after I discovered my boyfriend had been cheating on me and I broke up with him, I became painfully aware of how popular we were. Without help from social media or the internet, the news of our breakup was on everyone's minds and lips; the next morning, the moment I stepped on campus with my puffy eyes from crying the night before, they all entered my personal space. Full exposure was something I wasn't used to, nor did I like it. In retrospect, with no cell phone to hide my face in, as well as countless "condolence hugs," "random rants," and being emotionally dumped on by others who were angry for me, it's no surprise that I was completely exhausted by the end of the first day of our breakup. The days after were filled with more of the same. People I didn't really know were checking on me, updating me, and, most notably, hitting on me. The pressure was real.

I finally broke down and shared my "school world" with my neighbor, who was in eleventh grade, and without warning, despite the fact that I was always fun loving and joking with her, I began to cry. She consoled me and we talked about what was going on with me. My heart was breaking and my tears continued to fall because, despite having done so in the past, I knew I could not take my ex back. We had broken up before, but never due to cheating or the suspicion of it. This breakup was different, this would be the end. But even as I thought that, I couldn't help but wonder how I would say no when he came back—because I knew he would. I knew it wasn't possible to stay angry forever, but I felt so many things, and they felt stronger than anger. I just wasn't quite sure what I *was* feeling.

I don't remember telling my mom about our breakup right away, but I'm pretty sure I must have, because she and I were close. I didn't tell her everything about my relationships, but we would share gossip. While the breakup was hard, it started out very juicy, considering I discovered his cheating by secretly overhearing him on a three-way call, the early version of today's conference call. Nevertheless, eventually she and I sat down to discuss things, and I brought her up to speed on everything. And then she said it: "If you allow a man to come in and out of your life, he'll never respect you." There was the word that would change my self-esteem forever: RESPECT. I wasn't just angry at my boyfriend, I felt disrespected by him. I felt disrespected by his treatment of me and by the conversation I had overheard. After being together for over a year, he said he loved me, but he didn't have respect for me.

As I had expected, he eventually attempted to communicate with me by sending a mutual friend to test the waters of reconciliation. While I listened to our friend's voice in person, my mind was replaying my mom's words, reminding me that he would NEVER respect me if I allowed him to come back into my life as my boyfriend. So instead of agreeing to meet with my former boyfriend so he could attempt to reconcile with me, I gave our friend a different message to deliver. I told that friend, "Tell him I will take him back when hell freezes over." I know it was corny, but it was the eighties. I rattled off a few more indignant comments, like "how dare he send you instead of speaking to me himself." Eventually, we did speak in person. He apologized and we moved on as friends. This experience was the beginning of my process of identifying how I would love and expect to be loved in the future. I learned what type of treatment I deserved and how to determine if a person was respecting me and was therefore worth me spending my time with.

People become friends for various reasons in the seasons of life; I believe that friendships have purpose and are often important to our individual development. One girl (who I will here call Anne) and I became friends, and eventually best friends, because we had a shared interest in attending dances. While we were complete opposites in many areas, such as style of dress, academic goals, and the groups we hung out with, we celebrated our similarities, like our love for boys and parties, and respected our differences—or so I thought.

Predictably, we met guys at the parties who became more than dance partners, a boyfriend for me and a love interest, what we would call today a hookup, for her. I was a virgin, and she was not, so our respective partners were appropriate choices for each of us—again, so I thought. Ultimately, Anne and her guy's situation ran its course and they parted ways, while my relationship continued. Strangely, though, my boyfriend seemed to develop a strong disdain for my bestie. After repeated requests by him that I not bring her, along with inquiries about our friendship and why we were friends anyway, it came out that they had been sexual partners behind my back. I was told the truth accidentally by one of his friends, who I tricked into telling me one night on the phone. My boyfriend then called and confessed, with details, angst, anguish, and anger. He had been seduced, he said. He regretted everything, especially hurting me, and apologized repeatedly. My bestie, though, took a different and disappointing approach: denial.

As is typically the case, EVERYONE in our friend group knew about them betraying me but me, and they kept the secret. However, once the secret was exposed, they all were talking—except my bestie. I explained to her that her unwillingness to admit the truth was disrespectful to our friendship and hurtful. She maintained that what she was being accused of was untrue, even though I knew it was true. I really loved my friend and would have forgiven her, as the boyfriend didn't mean that much to me. But I could not offer forgiveness that was not requested; it would have been disrespectful to myself. I knew that I should not allow a person to be in my life who didn't have enough respect for me to admit when they had wronged me. No respect equaled no friendship. She didn't respect me, so I stopped being her bestie. Of course, my former boyfriend's behavior was also disrespectful, even with his claims of being seduced, so he was dropped, too. Civility was maintained amongst all involved, and we became associates instead of friends and kept it moving.

It is important to personal development and the establishment of personal standards to take the time to explore the emotions one experiences during and after separating from a partner or friend. While you are living the experience, it can be hard to separate emotions from facts. Therefore, having people in your life who you know love, respect, and support your personal standards is vital. For example, if your personal standard includes maintaining your virginity, try to be friends with others who respect you and your decision, whether they share that value or not. Likewise, you should offer the same respect to others. A person who respects him or herself will have standards that reflect having positive self-esteem, which is different than being judgmental and/or self-righteous. Having self-respect is not about being demanding, it is simply knowing what is right for you, what isn't, and why.

Shortly after high school, I met a guy who was cool, a friend type I thought. We hung out casually at first, grabbing food together and so forth. Eventually, he asked to take me out to dinner and I agreed. But on the day of our date, the time he was scheduled to arrive had come and gone and I had not heard from him. Approximately thirty minutes later than we had scheduled to meet, he called and said he was on his way. I told him he was late and, because I had not heard from him, I had made other plans. We went back and forth about the need on his part to have called earlier (as his failure to do so was clear disrespect for my time) and about that being the reason I scheduled something else to do. He was heated and called me an expletive under his breath while hanging up. I laughed, called my girl, and went to her house. We agreed that the behavior he demonstrated on the phone was out of character for him (as by that point we had interacted for a couple of months and knew his character), but she supported my stance that he should've called earlier. A little later that evening, I decided to check my voicemails—and he had called again. He said that he had driven to Los Angeles, thirty minutes from his home, hoping to see me after I was done with my plans. He apologized for not calling sooner and asked me to give him a call when I could. He sounded very sincere, so I called and we got together that evening. We had a great time, and he is now my husband of over twenty years.

During the early years of our relationship, when we met up with other couples and friends, we would often tell stories of how we got together, so of course our "first date" stories would always come up. For us, that was a subsequent dinner date. However, there was an occasion when my husband began to speak of another "first date" with me that he credits as being the experience that changed him and the course of our relationship. He called it the "she made other plans" date.

Since there are two sides to a story, I would tell our stories from my perspective and then he would do the same. However, when he began to tell his version of "she made other plans," I was pleasantly surprised when he added more to his version than just the facts as I knew them.

He explained to our friends that he was heated on the phone that night because he had never before experienced someone telling him that they had made other plans when he was late. And while he was surprised and then pissed off, he was also impressed by my ability to maintain my standards and demand respect. He had agreed that he should have called once I said it, but had tripped up on the fact that I was TELLING him and REFUSING to see him because he was late. He said, "I had never dealt with a girl who had standards she stuck to," and therefore wanted to get to know me. So, he called me, left a message with an apology, and waited to see if I would allow him to still see me that night.

By that time in my life I had become pretty familiar with identifying behaviors or treatment from others that was seated in respect or disrespect, and equally comfortable saying *no* without hesitation to treatment that I did not want or deserve. I understood that my new friend wasn't trying to be shady, he was just used to assuming that he could be very late for a date without calling and still just show up as if nothing was wrong. During the encounter, the later it got, the more nervous I became, because I knew I would have a decision to make that could impact our friendship and/or potential relationship. The decision was, do I allow him to just arrive late and bring it up during our outing, or make other plans and risk being viewed as difficult, and basically facilitate a change in direction for us? I obviously chose the latter, but it was tough. Not tough because I liked him so much, but tough because I was putting myself first, and hoped that he would too. I knew it was the right thing to do, to lead with respect, but I wasn't sure if he would be mature enough to not only take responsibility for his words then and in the future, but to then also not be childish and hold a grudge. I remembered that my first loyalty was to myself, no matter what or with whom. His tardiness created an opportunity for the both of us to take a peek into the character of the person who we were planning to maybe date in the future. Once I acknowledged that fact, it was necessary for me to be willing to see who I was really considering spending time with that evening and after, even if my feelings got hurt in the process. As fate would have it, he was thinking along the same lines, and although it may have been uncomfortable at first, he responded by showing he respected me and my time by acknowledging, apologizing, and making the adjustment.

Dear Daughters:

Mastering your own approach in determining who is allowed to "come in and out of your life" takes time, experience, and self-reflection, among other things. However, my mom's advice, "If you allow a man to come in and out of your life, he'll never respect you," planted the seed that shifted my focus in all my relationships, both personal and professional. It is my hope that each of you will be careful to pay attention to who and what you allow to enter and exit your life.

A person's actions speak louder than their words, so pay close attention to what is said and what is done. A person can claim to be a best friend or to love you, but if they never show up for you when needed, or don't take responsibility for missteps in the friendship or relationship, you may need to reevaluate the value you place on that relationship.

Never stay in a relationship or friendship because of obligation or charity. If your gut tells you to move on from a relationship or association, do it. If you do the work to know yourself and what your goals are, you will be able to truly see the hearts of others, and even if that proves to be difficult, you can still evaluate their actions.

Lastly, surround yourselves with others who will encourage and empower you to be your best self, but who will also tell you the truth, even when it's tough to say. The experiences I shared are just a few examples of instances where I have had to put myself first at different times in my life. Each of you will experience moments like these, where what a person is saying doesn't line up with what or who they are showing you. I want you to have the courage to choose yourselves. Surrounding yourselves with a strong village of friends is necessary for the times when you may feel weak and are considering making a decision that doesn't honor you, as they will remind you of who you want to be.

Journal Page

A Daughter's Handbook

Dear Jefferionna,

I love you so much, and I want you to remember these simple words: Love yourself, and always put effort into yourself; you define you. Teach others how to love and respect you by showing them in your own actions toward yourself. Be honest, be true, and keep your word.

Mental health is very important, and you need to keep yourself in a great mental and emotional state. Your inner happiness will radiate to the outside of you, never the other way around.

Keep your hygiene up and dress yourself nicely every day; it will make you feel good.

Know who you are in Christ and have no doubt that God is real and he loves you. You are wonderfully and fearfully made in his image. He has empowered you with gifts and talents, and because of that, there is nothing too hard for you to do if you put actions toward your intentions. Use your gifts and talents in church, study the Bible, and pray every day. I can't stress enough how important a good prayer life is.

If you ever need help when I am not around, find yourself women like your grandmother who will encourage you and make you better.

You do not have to tolerate violence. Someone who loves you should not hurt you. When someone loves you, they will uplift you and want to be around you. You do not have to take anything from anyone.

Financially, I advise you *not* to spend all your money. Save for the future.

The characteristics and qualities that you like in men today, you will probably not like ten years from now. This is because as you grow, your desires and needs will change.

Trust yourself to make good decisions. Take care of yourself first. You must fill yourself up first and then use the overflow to take care of others.

Be strong within yourself, mentally, physically, emotionally, and spiritually. And there's nothing you can do that will ever stop me from loving you. I want the best for you.

So remember, you are somebody and you are in control of your own destiny. Praise God at all times and know you can do all things in Christ.

Love,
Mom (Anjanette)

Dear Leila and Parker,

I want you to know that I love you both so very much. I am so grateful that God has entrusted me to be your mommy. Growing up, I never thought that I would ever have children. Frankly, I saw how much my mother struggled with me and my siblings and it scared the heck out of me.

I never wanted things to be hard for us. Shoot, truth be told, we haven't had it easy by any stretch of the imagination. We've shared some amazing moments and some situations that brought me to my knees, but I need you to know that I am giving you my very best. The Bible says that God uses all things for our good, and for this reason I try to always remind you two little beauties to see the lesson in every "L," every loss, we've ever taken. I promise you, it's for our good, even if it doesn't *feel* good in the moment.

I'm happy and blessed to share this journey with you both. You girls keep me on my toes (and my knees) and you teach me something new about myself every day. One day, you'll have little eyes peering up at you, observing how you handle a bully at work, how you set boundaries, how you love, the way you run your home, and even how you allow others to treat you. It's my prayer that in those moments, you will hear my voice and remember the training and instruction that I gave you when you were younger. The word of God says in

Proverbs 22:6 to "Train up a child in the way he should go: and when he is old, he will not depart from it." Stay the course, babies!

Finally, I want you both to know that I believe in you and I will always be here for you. You are always in my thoughts, in my prayers, and in my heart. I challenge you to go farther than I have ever gone and to do greater things than I will ever do. I encourage you to live a life that you can be proud of, a life that honors God. Never compromise your dignity or self-respect for anyone and always give thanks. I'll leave you with this: "Trust in the Lord with all your heart and lean not on your own understanding; in all your ways submit to him, and he will make your paths straight." (Proverbs 3:5–6)

I love you with everything I have in me.

Hugs,
Mommy (April)

Dear Lil' Ashley,

I hope and pray that I have been a great example to you of how to live and love, how to treat people, and how to be a good person, no matter what others do or what life throws at you. As soon as you were conceived I began compiling pictures, writing letters, and making videos so that you could see what my life was like, as well as witness your emergence into my life through your dad's and my eyes. It would take a lifetime to tell you everything I ever wanted to say, and even then it wouldn't be enough. My wish is for you to be happy and healthy and be the best person you can be.

I spent so many nights dreaming of you. So many hours praying for you. So many years preparing myself so that I could be the best possible mother to you and could lay a foundation that would give you the best possible start to life that I could provide. All of this was before circumstances ever occurred to cause there to be a you. God has a plan for your life and I planned and prepared for you. Never ever feel alone, unloved, or unwanted. God is always with you, and you will always carry me with you in your heart everywhere you go.

You are a very special person with immense value and you are the biggest blessing of my life. I waited over thirty-seven years to create you and prayed and prayed for you long before I ever met your dad. You are beautiful, smart, talented, and loved more than you can ever imagine. You are a mix of some of the best qualities, characteristics, and genetics there are, and you and your personality take everything to a level that far surpasses the best I could have ever dreamed of.

You are unique and I always want you to embrace your power and individuality and never feel like you have to be a part of or conform to the ideas of a group or person. NEVER change who you are or the way you think for ANYBODY. Not everyone is going to like you and you don't have to be everyone's friend, but ALWAYS remember to treat everybody with kindness and respect. Be humble, but don't let people run over you or devalue you. Always know and remember your worth, and let your light shine and your accomplishments speak for themselves.

Embrace life and what it has to offer. Education is key; make it your goal to never stop learning. Keep your eyes and ears open, and if you truly want something, put your mind, effort, and heart into it and make it happen. As long as you are able to take care of yourself and your responsibilities, let yourself live your life, go to new places, have great adventures, and collect awesome memories.

Make it a point to always take care of your health—mind, body, and spirit. Wherever you go, always know that God is with you. Remember to pray as I have taught you and to give thanks and praise to God in good times and bad. You only have one body, and it is very important that you eat well, exercise, and be extremely careful with what you put in your body and who you choose to come into contact with. Know who you are and what your triggers and buttons are, and make sure to distance yourself from people and situations that threaten to steal your peace or joy. Your mind is one of your strongest weapons. Stay focused; set goals and work diligently toward them. Remember to stay true to yourself and stand up for what you believe in, no matter what. Do not let your voice be silent.

Always, ALWAYS let your word be your bond and understand that it is okay to say NO. In life you will end up hurting people, but make sure you never harm people intentionally. Know that sometimes—most times—it's more important to listen than to talk. You don't have to go around talking yourself up or bragging to everyone how great you are. But please understand that there are times when you may need to toot your own horn. Do not be ashamed of your background, heritage, or any advantage or disadvantage you have had in comparison to others. Treat everyone with the kindness and respect that you would want in return.

I know our family dynamic is crazy. Remember, though, that if you tell everyone what is going on in your life, you will have that same number of opinions of why you should or shouldn't do something. When talking to people, listen to what is said, take what may be of value, and the rest file someplace else or discard. DO NOT live your life for someone else or stifle your dreams because someone tells you that something is impossible. As long as your responsibilities are met, it's completely okay to blaze your own trail. With all that said, there is a lot of love in our family, and no matter how dysfunctional or untraditional it is, you are surrounded by love.

I wish I had a million years to hug you and hold you and shield you from every hurt, pain, test, or trial. Know that you come from strength and are strong. Every tough time you go through will teach you something. Learn from it and don't repeat your mistakes. Take deep breaths when you need to and know that no matter how hard things may seem, everything is going to be okay.

You have everything inside of you that you need to be amazing beyond belief. Let your light shine! I love you unconditionally, immensely, and eternally.

Love,
Mom (Ashley)

Dear Jana,

I just want to let you know how much I love you and how extremely proud I am of who you have become. You have grown into a fine woman who isn't afraid to allow the world to see who you are. You have always been bold enough to dream and challenge yourself to do and be better. Oh, how you inspire your momma!

As you're going along your way in your journey, continue to be the awesome woman you are. Know that, no matter what anyone says, you are amazing. If someone tries to bring you down or tries to make you feel like you're not awesome, it is because they can't see your awesomeness, not because you don't possess it.

I've always told you how beautifully and wonderfully made you are. You are made in God's image and are the apple of his eye. He loves you, and Mommy loves you too.

I know that you'll eventually marry; just don't rush into anything. Take your time and pray about it. There are people in your corner who will hold you accountable to the decisions you make, people like your dad, Grandma, your brother, Uncle Gene, Elder Betty, Elaine, and Aprille. All of them are capable of answering your tough questions. Don't be afraid to ask for help, and if you see warning signs, take notice of them and then choose what is best for you.

Never compromise your values. Believe in them and stand on them, in social, intimate, and business settings.

Believe in yourself; stand strong and tall. When it comes to business, do what is good for you, no matter how much money is offered to you to do otherwise. Look and see if it is a business deal that will compliment what you want, who you are, and where you are going. If it is not, it isn't the business deal for you. Don't be afraid to tell them no.

Don't be afraid to speak up. You are a voice that needs to be heard. Say what God gives you, no matter what it is.

Now, when you become a parent, make sure that you let your kids see you laugh. Teach them cultural things. Don't ever allow yourself to be lost in your family and children. Make sure they see you having fun, and travel with them on vacations so you all can see the world. You will be their leader, so teach them to shine wherever they are.

Where money is concerned, always be a wise investor as well as a good steward over it. You have learned principles of how to save, spend, and pay your tithes. Additionally, make sure that you do these four things:

1. When it comes to investments, make sure they multiply your money.

2. Never make the deal personal.

3. Don't be afraid to get out if the deal is not growing your money.

4. If you make a mistake, stop, reevaluate your decision, and start over.

I love you Jana, always know that. Your family will be your biggest supporter, so if you need to talk about anything, don't hold it in, talk to us. Also, Lois is just a phone call away. The love she has for God and you will give you great guidance.

Love,
Mom (Dee)

Dear Jelani,

First, let me say that miracles do not happen every day, yet on October 2, 2003, a miracle happened to me and for me. You saved me more than you will ever know. My life became yours. The moment I laid eyes on you, I knew that nothing and no one could come before you. Even though I was coming from a place of infertility, not knowing if I would ever be able to leave a legacy, you came along and proved everyone wrong. There are many jewels of knowledge that I've gifted you on your journey to womanhood; it is my desire that you utilize them for good and continue to build upon them. You are beautiful. You were one of the cutest babies I've ever seen, if not THE cutest baby I've ever seen. You are cute but also serious, and that's okay, because you get that from me.

To say that I am proud would be an understatement, because it does not express what I feel about who you have become. I want you to continue to be Jelani, that mighty warrior who stands up for what she believes in. Continue to advocate for yourself, but remember that not every battle deserves your energy, and not every battle deserves a fight with others as well as yourself. This world is not for the faint of heart or the weak of mind, so ground yourself, because you will need it to remain connected to me and with me, as well as with all the other women who have come before you. Walk barefoot, sing, laugh, cry, travel, and love hard. Always remain connected to the masculine energy that I manifested for you. He appears physically on this earth as your brother; although he is younger, if ever a storm should come, he will walk alongside you holding the umbrella.

Take the road less traveled. Sometimes it will be dark, lonely, cold, slippery, and scary, but that's okay. Just understand that all of those obstacles exist because only the bold make the choice to take that journey. Don't get discouraged; keep walking ahead, head high, shoulders back, confident, and secure, with full knowledge of yourself. Ask questions; only fools remain silent. Seek knowledge in order to understand, but master knowledge of thyself first. Become one with the universe and allow it to guide you; ask for what you need. Meditate; eat well. Remember all of the things that you witnessed in me throughout your life. Be kind to your bodily temple so that it gives you an abundance of years in which to use it. Take care of your emotional state, as it's a must.

Stay connected to your aunts and uncle. Stay connected to the whole family. Allow them to love you, care for you, and help steer you in the right direction. Your Auntie Gina is the most caring, loving woman I know; respect her as you would me. Although she's hard on you, she loves you very much. From day one she has been there teaching you good (and sometimes bad) things. I mean, come on, she was a teenager when I had you, but all in all, she means well, and she will take you where you need to go. Know that I love you and always will; if I've ever caused you pain it was not intentional, but always part of a bigger lesson that we both needed to learn. My daughter, my life, my mini-me, my sunshine, Hollywood, in the rain, in the snow, in the summer it's me and you. You are my why, my because, my must, my muse, my stretchmarks. Remain above even when you are feeling down; remember, never sink; float, stand, walk, run, and soar.

Love,
Mommy (Ereena)

Dear Alana, Genise, and Kaaliyah,

I want you girls to know that I love you more than anything in the world and I feel so proud and honored to be your mother. I often joke around and say that it seems as if someone took my personality and split it into three separate beings and now I'm raising myself, but I also recognize that you girls are all unique individuals and I look forward to watching you mature into the young ladies that God intended you to be.

I want to give you a few pieces of advice to help you live by and to guide your life. First of all, make good decisions. Your decisions have the ability to impact your life for either good or for bad; you get to choose. Also, choose your own path in life. I want you to figure out why God put you on this Earth. Once you figure it out, chase after it as if your soul is on fire. Be a go-getter; if something doesn't exist, create it. You don't have to wait for somebody to make something happen for you; make it happen for yourself. Watch out for distractions; a lot of times when we are chasing our goals, or when we are walking in our purpose, we find ourselves dealing with a lot of distractions. Some distractions come in the form of fun, while others come in the form of drama; deal with them accordingly. Also, know that your health is your wealth. If you aren't taking care of yourself emotionally, physically, or mentally, it's hard to live out your full potential, so make sure that you make your health a priority. Be financially responsible. This is a big one, because a lot of the time, when we think about our finances, we think only about our current financial situation. We don't really think about how we have the ability to help others and to impact future generations if we are financially responsible right now. Also, live a life of servitude; give back and be there for others like someone was there for you.

We live in a society that makes us feel as if we're not enough. We're not pretty enough. We're not strong enough. We're not smart enough. I want you to always know that you are enough, and there is no reason for you to feel insecure, because God already validated you before you were even thought of. Everything that you need in life is already inside of you. You just have to reach down deep and access that part of you. Speak positively about yourself. Stand up for yourself. Use empowering techniques such as *I am* statements to help you get through those hard times, and never give up, because you can do it. Create boundaries; when we talk about relationships, it is very important to create boundaries, to know the things that you will and will not tolerate. Abuse is never okay, no matter how much you love that person or they claim to love you.

Everyone should be better for knowing you. I want you to add value to others and hold on to relationships that add value to you. Relationships have the ability to change your life, so it's very important that you watch who you give your time and energy to. I also want you to trust your instincts and know that if something doesn't feel right, it's probably not right.

Finally, remember that knowledge is power. I want you to read as much as you can and be lifelong learners. The moment you stop learning is the moment you stop growing. I hope that this advice helps you and guides you, but also know that I'm here for you and that you have a community of people who love you and are rooting for you. Tap into our knowledge and learn from our life experiences.

Love,
Mommy (Ginca)

Dear Jozalynn,

There are five areas I really want you to focus on and take with you during the rest of your life. I want to make sure to get you the tools you need to move forward. Those areas are the mental, the physical, your dreams and emotions, the spiritual, and your finances.

MENTAL

As you know, I'm a therapist—and guess what, I'm going to always advocate for you to get your own therapist. It's okay to cry, it's okay to be sad, it's okay to be angry, and so forth, but it's also okay to let go of those things and give them to someone else to help you process, so you can move forward in life and do the beautiful things you're meant to do.

PHYSICAL

Stay healthy. There's so much stuff going on in our family tree. There's asthma, there's diabetes, just "being black", there's heart disease, there's all these things. So stay active. You live in Chicago. We have a beautiful lakefront. If you want to move to California, there's a big ocean right there as well. Wherever you go, just make sure you're taking the time to stay active, keep your body right, keep your skin tight, and just keep everything glowing, healthy and flowing. You know, stay away from the hot chips. I know they're delicious, but don't eat those, because they're not good for you. Yes, soul food is great too, but you need green leafy vegetables, things like that, because when you get old, stuff breaks down and stuff doesn't feel the same. My knees hurt every day and I'm not even forty yet. I have to get my diet right, so I want you to also make sure you're eating healthy.

DREAMS AND EMOTIONS

I want you to strive to be whatever you want to be. You want to be an OB-GYN? You do that! If you want to have your own lip-gloss line, you do that! You want to act? Do it! There's so many things you want to do and that you can do. Often, people don't get their break until they're thirty, forty, or fifty, so don't let that stop you from dreaming and exploring and being whatever! You know Mommy has your back! I love you and I just thank you for being you, for being honest and already a go-getter. You're strong, you're motivated, and you kind of want to be like me, but BETTER, and that wouldn't be bad. But who can blame you? I'm pretty awesome. So dream big, please. Dream big, dream big, dream big. You can do whatever you set your mind to.

SPIRITUAL

In all fairness, everything goes to the Man upstairs. God has been taking care of me from day one! He's gotten me through a lot of things, so I want you to just stay focused on his word and become closer in your relationship with him. It's not about whether you go to church every single day. Yes, things like that are important, but it's more about the relationship, and I want you to make sure you stay close to God and keep him in your heart. Read your Bible; read things that are spiritual in nature. Stay focused and clear with where you want to go, and don't be afraid to ask. He does miracles. He is able to move mountains, so whatever you need—ask! And no, God's not a genie in a bottle, so don't think that if you just pray, pray, pray that it's going to be easy, because that's not how it works. But if you need him, God's got your back at all times.

FINANCES

Do not, do not, do not go out into this world and expect things to be handed to you. You have to work hard, but also be smart. That means making sure you're saving, making sure you're keeping your credit. You know what? Buy a house at age twenty-one when you get out of college! You know what? Do those things that are going to put you in a financial space where you don't have to struggle or cry because you don't know how you'll eat tomorrow.

Take all these things to heart, baby girl, and you're going to fly! Thank you for being you!

Love,
Mommy (Jennifer)

Dear Kayla,

I love you so much. You have been the absolute joy of my life from the moment I found out I was pregnant with you. You have given me so much hope for my future. I want you to know I'm proud of you.

There's nobody on this earth that I love nearly as much as you. You are my legacy—you are my inspiration and my reason to push so hard and never give up, so I can make life amazing; you are never my excuse not to. Thank you for allowing me to be your guide through this world.

As I think of the legacy I want to leave you, here are some vital things I want you to know:

MENTAL

Read! Read everything; from the back of the cereal box to everything in the bookstore. Read personal development books, everything by John Maxwell, and financial books by Robert Kiyosaki, Patrice Washington, and Tiffany "The Budgetnista" Aliche. Study your Bible so you can understand it, even if you have to start with a children's Bible and use it for twenty years before you graduate up. That's perfectly acceptable. You don't have to start off with the King James version.

The Obstacle Is the Way by Ryan Holiday, *The Secret* by Rhonda Byrne, and *The Power of Vulnerability* by Brene Brown are all amazing books that impacted my life. Read about your history, Black history and women's history.

Watch your language. Choose your words carefully. Don't say "I have to go to school," excitedly say "I get to go to school." Training yourself to say "I get to" instead of "I have to" is a life changer.

PHYSICAL

You are beautiful, baby. Flash your winning smile and extend your hand to everyone you meet. A good handshake speaks to your confidence, so practice it on everyone you meet. Be firm, be direct, and look people in their eyes when you speak to them. And when you ask someone "how are you doing?" stand there and listen while they answer.

Get plenty of exercise. Keep your body moving, because that keeps us healthy. Roots Nutrition and Nature's Sunshine are great places to get herbs, and apple cider vinegar is great for keeping your immune system together.

EMOTIONAL

Emotional intelligence is essential to life. Process your feelings. Think things through and respond accordingly. I have spent a lot of time in my life being reactive, and I want you to instead really process how you feel about all things. Ask yourself, "what do I think about that?" or "how do I feel about that?" If you need one, get a therapist to help you deal with any past trauma and a life coach to help you move forward into your future.

SPIRITUAL

God loves you so much that after he created the heavens and the earth he still saw a need for you here. That means that there is something he wants done, and you, Kayla, are the one he has chosen to do it. Discover that purpose and fulfill it.

Pray as much as you can and as hard as you can. Choose a personal relationship with God over religion. A relationship with God teaches discipline and brings your flesh under subjection. So do what you have to do, and then you can do what you want to do.

Be nice to everyone, and remember, "kind people are our kind of people." Before you speak, ask yourself if what you are about to share is true, kind, and necessary. If the answers are all yes, ask yourself another set of questions: Does this need to be said? Does this need to be said by me? Does this need to be said by me right now?

FINANCIAL

Money provides options. Don't let people tell you that you're not supposed to charge for your services. If you have learned a skill, monetize it. But here is something super important about money: don't focus on saving money, focus on creating more money.

PROFESSIONAL

Think outside the box. You don't have to go to college if you don't want to, but if you don't, you definitely must have a way to create the income a degree would have brought you. If you choose to start a business, get a business coach that has a great track record for the business you want.

LIFE

You do have to be a productive citizen. You cannot be a burden to society, so you have to get up and make life happen. Create a goal list and a vision board and pursue them! I want you to become a woman who is well grounded and able to make integrity-based decisions. Hold your independence until you need to be interdependent, but if at all possible, avoid being dependent on people if you can help it, because you don't want to be a burden or oppressed.

LOVE

Don't be afraid of heartbreak. Don't be afraid to express yourself and be vulnerable. Learn to have emotional intelligence in your relationships. That means learning to say "I love you and I am afraid of losing you" instead of "Who is that? What's her name? Why is she calling you? Do you like her? Do you want to break up?" etc. You may laugh at this, but only because it is true. Learn to communicate with the man of your choosing.

LEGACY

You have a great legacy inside of you. You come from kings and queens, slaves, soldiers, civil rights leaders, front line defenders of women's rights, law enforcement, teachers, politicians, entrepreneurs, and all around good people. When an obstacle gets in your way, the obstacle becomes the new path to success. BULLDOZE IT!

Love,
Mommy (Kiana)

Dear DeNarae and DaeLynn,

This was the second hardest thing to do in my life. I hope to let this drive me to teach you as much as possible every day, so I can know you are aware that I love you more than air. All the greatness I hold stems from the love I have for you and have felt from you. The pure love in your eyes made me see myself. It let me know I needed to learn to truly love myself better. It was such an important lesson to learn so late in life. I couldn't let that happen to my daughters. So, like I said, I will feel I've failed if you're not greater than me. I strive to give you a higher start as you stand on my shoulders.

Knowing I've made many mistakes, I would like to give you the biggest, most sincere apology for ever hurting you. I love you so much. Please trust and believe that I've never intentionally hurt you. I am truly sorry.

That being said, I want you to trust and believe in yourselves. Know that you are great. Know that you are capable of having and doing anything and everything that you want to do. Make sure you choose good, because your power works whichever way you lead it. God IS good, so please always choose good, even in the so-called difficult times, because life is really about working out issues. Without issues, growth is limited. Mental, physical, romantic, and financial growth come from having problems, whether they were someone else's that they solved and you learned from, or your own that you figured out. Face issues when they come as life's challenges. Accept the mindset that you are a winner and triumph. The action is simple, but you have to trust and believe in yourself. I know you can. Remember to first love yourselves, and let that be your guide in relationships: love doesn't hurt. Love doesn't hurt your mind. Love doesn't hurt your body. Love doesn't hurt your soul. And love certainly doesn't hurt your bank account! You may often hear throughout your lives a quote by Maya Angelou: "When somebody shows you who they are, believe them." In other words, don't lie to yourselves for the sake of another. It is incredibly damaging to your love for yourself; if you can't trust yourself to be honest, then who can you trust? No one is worth damage to your self-esteem!

Any moment is a good time to reevaluate. No decision has to be permanent. Love yourselves enough to forgive yourselves and reroute your course. You got this.

For guidance beyond myself, I would direct you to Auntie Catrina; I trust her with everything. Although I don't agree with her about everything, I know she will never steer you wrong. Also, look to the women that helped ground and direct me, my god-sister Desi and my cousin Judy. These women will keep you straight and give it to you real, with love and encouragement. I trust them deeply and their discernment is something you can always count on, to bring you down when you're on the ledge, to build you up when you need to get on that platform, or to celebrate with you when you need a fan. You are also blessed to have two amazing, wise, and empathetic big brothers that love you and will always have your back, even when you get on their nerves. You each have a great sister in your corner that loves you and wants the best for you. She is your first, best friend. Let her be there for you, and remember to be there for her. The four of you make an amazing team (I'm just saying).

Everything is gonna be okay, always know that. The sun rises every day, and that is always your second blessing of the day, after the breath of life. So know you wake up blessed every day. Know that you're loved. Know you matter. You are so amazing.

I love and admire you, Miss DeNarae Stewart. I love and admire you, Miss DaeLynn Stewart. I'm so proud to be your mother. I am doubly blessed to be the mother of two uniquely awesome young ladies. It's an honor to be your mother and I thank you from my soul. I leave you with infinite, too tight hugs and the sweetest slobbery mommy kisses. I love you more than air.

Love,
Mommy (Mara)

Dear Destiny,

Oh, how I wish I were half as smart as you are when I was your age. You are so bright, intelligent, kind, helpful, and loving to a fault. You've always been the first to step up and help and you never want to see anyone hurting. I am over the moon proud of you, and even more proud to be your mom. I just want to take a few moments to highlight your amazingness through my eyes and also give you some valuable tools to carry with you throughout life. You are a light. You shine bright like a diamond and you are always encouraging others to shine their brightness in your presence. I want you to know that even during the times that seem the darkest, your light is still there. Turn to God first to connect you with your inner light. He will always guide and show you exactly where you need to be.

My love, you are powerful. Your personal power, your strength and desire to let nothing stop you from reaching your goals, is something that many don't ever learn they have and that most your age haven't yet discovered. Use your power to help others. Show them, especially young women, how important it is to feel their own power, their own value and self-worth. The power within you is something no one can take away from you, and I want you to never give it away. It's part of who you are, who you have grown to be, and it's a beautiful part of you because you share it in the presence of others.

When it comes to trust, you get to trust yourself. You don't have to, but you get to. It begins with trusting your intuition. This is the place where God speaks to your spirit; it is your truth. I'm so proud to be a witness of the intuitive journey you are on, and more importantly, I'm honored through my own intuitive healing. It has helped me connect with you and rebuild our relationship in the most genuine ways.

This mother-daughter relationship that we have is priceless and precious. You have always been such an appreciative child and you have grown into an appreciative young lady. This is one of the qualities I deeply admire about you. Be grateful every day. Each day gives you something to be grateful for. I think of how grateful I am for you and your brothers. Give gratitude for the simple things, like electricity, water, the flowers outside, grass, and dirt. These are things that we normally don't pay attention to. As crazy as it sounds, be grateful for the things that annoy you, because it's an indication that you're able to feel, which is yet another thing to be grateful about. Remember to be grateful even for the things that have upset or hurt you, because they have given you the opportunity to grow and heal and discover more about yourself.

Never be afraid to feel or be afraid of what you feel. Your feelings are real, and no one should tell you different. Don't allow others to put a timeframe on how long you should feel something. In order to heal something in you, you must feel it. You must acknowledge it's there. You will experience a wide range of emotions, and I pray I have given you some of the tools that you need, in combination with your own life lessons, to get through any or all of them. Your spirit is so beautiful, calming, and magnetic. It carries that uniqueness in your own personal relationship with God at any given moment. All you have to do is close your eyes, connect to your spirit, and listen to God. Your spirit will never present doubt. It will never lie to you and it is never to be compromised. People can feel the authenticity in your energy because of the purity of your spirit.

There are three things I want you to carry with you every day for the rest of your life. One, fall in love with yourself and love yourself first. Two, all of the answers to life's questions can be found in prayer and meditation. Three, all that you need in this life, God has already put in you. I love you from the core of my heart, my soul, and my spirit, and more than I could ever express in words. If you are making God happy, you will be happy, which will automatically make me happy. Thank you for learning from my greatness, my faults, my mistakes, and my truth. Now go out and live a beautiful life, my love.

Love,
Mom (Tasha)

Dear Breanna and Teyanna,

Mommy loves you both so very much. You two are the reason I wake up every morning and you are both the greatest joy and gift that God has blessed me with. You are the loves of my life. I want to give you both some key insights to live by that will help you grow.

First, I want to remind you of some very important women in our family whose examples you should live by. Grandma Stella was a woman of wisdom, a woman of faith. Even though Grandma Stella is no longer here with us, she is still a part of us through all the wisdom that she placed in us daily. A single mother of six children, who continued working even with snow coming up to her knees, she kept smiling and raised her children without needing assistance from the government or anyone else. I believe the most she ever made was six dollars an hour, and yet she was able to pay for two homes by herself and take care of her children.

Grandma Dorothy is another woman you should look to, a woman of true substance. After her divorce, she was able to start over by herself and rebuild. She's almost seventy-five years old now, even though she doesn't look like it; she doesn't look like what she's been through. So if you want to talk to someone about how to stay young and about having and building up your faith, go to Grandma Dorothy.

There is also my mother, your Grandma Gloria. She is a woman of true strength, a woman of faith. She daily thanks God for giving her the strength to wake up in the morning and for giving her the strength to endure everything she's been through. She doesn't show what she's been through, and she is a woman of fashion. Oh my gosh. She has over a hundred pairs of shoes, and outfits to match all hundred pairs of her shoes. If you want to talk to someone about fashion, if you need any tips on shoes, go to Grandma Gloria; she's the woman for you.

I also want to remind you of Auntie Toya; she has so much willpower, so much strength. When she was pregnant, she worked all the way until it was time for her to go into labor, making sure she had enough money saved up so she could pay for everything that she needed for her daughter without getting any assistance from anyone.

Finally, there is Auntie Tina. She is a woman who is good with her hands. She can build anything. She can do hair, she can crochet, she can draw, and she can write. If you want to build up your creativity, get Auntie Tina to help you

There are some true women of strength in our family; you can go to any of them at any time to help build you up or to help motivate you. All these amazing women of God will help you and push you in the right direction. When you feel like you're going the wrong way, call any one of these amazing women of God.

Always remember, I want you to live. I want you to enjoy life. You two are amazing women. Know that you are beautiful. Don't let anybody tell you differently. And if anybody tries to bring you down, just remember your mother's voice, saying that you can do anything that you want to. The sky is the limit. Always reach for the sky. Never give up on your dreams. If there is a big dream that you don't think you can accomplish, write it down. And as you write it down, speak it aloud, speak life into the atmosphere, because your words have power, and when you speak the atmosphere shifts. So write down the things that you want. As they come to pass, check them off from your list. Also remember to never settle for anything in life. Don't be in a relationship just to be in a relationship. Know that you can be anyone you want, so never settle, never ever settle; instead, continue to build.

Finally, I want to remind you to always read the Bible, because the Bible has everything you need and will go through in your life. If you need strength, the word is there. If you need faith, the word is there. If you need motivation, the word is there. Read the Bible. It's the best book for you and will feed you when you feel hungry.

Those are the key things I want to tell you for your life. Remember that, like a beautiful butterfly, you're just waiting to open, and when you open, you're going to fly. Keep rising to the top.

Love,
Mom (Tiffany)

My Dearest Daughters,

Life has been sweeter than I ever imagined because of each of you. I have laughed, cried, worried, dreamed, failed, and simply loved without limit because of you three, my babies. While your dad has been the ever-present, loving lion that worked hard to protect and "handle" the four of us, and to be all that each of us would need, I have tried to be the lioness.

As the lioness, I have tried to be an ever-loving presence, kind and supportive, yet ready in a moment to attack whoever I need to when I sense distress from one of my cubs. I hope that each of you feels my undying love and devotion to you every day of our lives together, as I truly love being with you every day of our lives! It is my expectation that you will love, encourage, respect, support, protect, and defend each other forever.

All of you, please strive to be a safe space for your sisters. It is my hope that each of you will always feel loved. Life will surely send moments of doubt and challenge to facilitate your growth, and during these times you will want to reach out in your distress. In my absence, girls, if your sister comes to mind, reach out to her and show her some love, some encouragement, or just some attention. Make time for each other regularly.

In the years to come, if your sister makes some decisions or finds herself in some circumstances that have caused her "crown" to be tilted, and you see it, straighten it for her; don't just let her walk through life looking crazy. Likewise, if you observe that her "slip is hanging," as my mom used to say when you're unknowingly exposing your business, point it out to her, as she may be unaware; after all, you know her momma taught her better. If her slip continues to hang, don't berate her, just recognize that she may be needing help. Help her get through whatever it is, and "pull her slip up" if you can. Try to be kind to one another. Take life one moment at a time and just love each other.

I am proud of the young ladies you are and even more proud of the amazing women I know you will become. Believe in yourselves, your abilities to achieve whatever you put your mind to, your intelligence, and most of all your gut or intuition when you're making decisions. And believe in your sisters . . . always! Thank you for choosing me to be your mom—I've cherished every minute and I love you forever!

Love,
Mom (Yolanda)

Afterword

In this competitive market of life coaches, authors, and inspirational and motivational speakers, only a few will ultimately rise to and stay at the top. They are successful because they are truthful, are good listeners, and respect the space of their clients. They have the grit, poise, and purpose to rise above the fakes. And if you read this book, you have just met one of the few coaches/speakers/authors that will rise to the top: Kiana Shaw.

Talk about a straight shooter! When I think back to the conversations I had with my mom, I remember that I had some questions after we had "the talk," but I was afraid my follow-up questions would make me look suspicious. Many of you have had that same experience about one subject or another, and in this book, Kiana and the other women take the time to be transparent and tell it like it is while still honoring that special relationship between mother and daughter. She guides the reader in a way that will allow them to have those tough conversations in a very natural way, on their own, as if they were talking to their younger self.

I have the pleasure of being "Bonus Mom" to Kiana Shaw. Traditionally known as a stepmother, Kiana was crystal clear when she informed me that there was nothing step about me. I love being her bonus mom.

Currently, I'm witnessing another special mother/daughter relationship. That's the one between Kiana and her daughter, Kayla. Kiana is loving but firm, and fair but tough. Kayla is a beautiful, vibrant, smart little girl with a strong will who is full of quick responses and never at a loss for words. I enjoy every time we visit, because I get to witness Kayla's growth and Kiana's imprint. They're both learning.

I hope that this book serves as a loving guide for all who read it, whether you are the mother or the daughter or both. May you be enlightened by the lessons these women share with you and yours for years to come.

Blessings,
Angela Gibson-Shaw
Kiana's Bonus Mom

About the Authors

KIANA SHAW

A master personal transformation coach, a four-time bestselling author, a public speaker, an award-winning podcast host, and a professional development coach, Kiana Shaw is the founder of LeadHERship Academy, a company designed to teach teen girls life, leadership, and empowerment skills to inspire, educate, and elevate them. She is also the creator of Mothers Raising Teen Daughters, a safe place for moms to express themselves while getting the tools and resources they need to bring love, joy, harmony, and supportive dialogue back to their homes.

Kiana is also a certified breakthrough parenting instructor and conducts classes both online and in groups to help parents regain their focus and ease the stress of day to day challenges with their kids. To date, Kiana has served over three thousand young ladies and their families, establishing herself as the go-to expert for all things teen girl related. Her success is powered by her authenticity and is rooted in her desire to see change in young women, a goal she has decided to be the agent of change for.

Kiana facilitates personal and professional development classes online and in person for all who desire to be proactive in the enrichment of their lives.

Drawing from her own experiences of sexual abuse, addiction, promiscuity, and low self-esteem, as well as other afflictions that plague teen girls, she has become a movement, using her knowledge to give freedom to young girls and women from all walks of life. Her life statement is simple: Vision without Action is Hallucination.

>Connect with Kiana at www.KianaShaw.com
>or email her at CoachKiana@gmail.com

ANJANETTE ROBINSON

Anjanette Robinson is a compassionate and dedicated spiritual teacher and prayer leader in ministry. She is a mentor who works with women and children, encouraging them to be spiritually, mentally, emotionally, and physically healthy individuals. She teaches them to love the essence of who they are in their community and to strive to be their best, living life to its fullest potential.

A mother of five by birth and with four bonus children, along with nine grandchildren, her passion is to build up blended families, one family at a time. She has been a wife for seventeen years and loves the family life. She was raised in Compton, California, and currently lives in Highland, California.

Contact her at anjanetterobinson1@gmail.com

APRIL MACK

April Mack is an overcoming survivor of domestic violence. Her victorious journey through abuse, single motherhood, low self-esteem, and depression has given her a passionate mission to educate, empower, and encourage vulnerable women and girls.

April is the founder of Empowering Our Daughters, an organization that teaches women and girls how to take back their own power. They learn that no matter what they've been through, they can overcome their past. Empowering Our Daughters encourages them not just to survive—but to thrive!

For more information on April Mack or her organization, please send an email to
EmpoweringOurDaughters@gmail.com

ASHLEY SHAW

Ashley Shaw is an author, public speaker, certified personal trainer, and health/wellness coach. Founder and owner of AshFit Solutions, she focuses on holistic, total body lifestyle transformation to ensure her clients are their best selves.

A tragic traffic accident ended her career in law enforcement as an LA County Deputy Sheriff, so Ashley had to reinvent her life. After neck and back surgery and re-teaching herself to walk, Ashley ultimately rehabilitated herself from using a walker to becoming a body competitor.

From that experience, AshFit Solutions was formed, and Ashley created a groundbreaking program to share her story of going from depression to triumph for the purpose of inspiring and motivating others, as well as to truly change lives through total fitness of the mind, body, and spirit.

Learn more at ashfitsolutions.com

DEE FRENCH

Dee French, CPC, has completed her bachelor's in theological studies and was awarded her honorary doctorate in religious education. She is CPR certified as well as being a financial advisor. But she doesn't stop there; in addition to the above, she is also a certified personal coach, a consultant, an author, a public speaker, and a marriage facilitator. She is indeed a highly knowledgeable woman of numerous talents. Being an entrepreneur has not stopped her love for empowering youth at APlaceofAbundance.org to become more productive and reach their full potential. In the past thirty years, Dee French has mentored and trained thousands of successful people in New York City and, recently, internationally. Through her mentoring and marriage facilitator programs, people can learn to walk in their purpose, thereby unlocking their hidden potential to live a life they love while helping those they serve.

Learn more at deefrench.com

EREENA GEORGE

An international bestselling author, a public speaker, a mom health educator, and a child advocate, Ereena George is the founder of The MOMific Group, a company created to assist moms in healing childhood trauma and improving their health so they can thrive, live in their purpose, foster better relationships, and raise productive children.

Drawing from her own experience of childhood trauma and depression, Ereena understands what it feels like to have these issues take over your life. After years of counseling, she decided to return to college to obtain her degree in child advocacy and policy so that she is able to help youth and families who may be experiencing that same trauma.

According to Ereena, "A healthy body gives way to a healthy mind. The first step in that transition begins with the foods we eat and how we think about ourselves. In order to become MOMific, one must use the proper nourishment."

Learn more at www.momific.life

GINCA LOVE

Ginca Love is a motivational speaker and the creator of the blog Love's Mosaic Life—but more importantly, she is the mother of three amazing daughters. She gave birth to her first daughter at the age of fifteen and her second daughter at sixteen. As a teen parent, she worked to provide the best life she could for her kids. After graduating, she joined the military and still proudly serves. As a childhood sexual abuse and domestic violence survivor and someone who has dealt with PTSD and depression, she has dedicated her life to helping others. Through her blog, she provides both encouragement and hope to others to pick up the pieces of their lives and create beauty out of brokenness. Ginca is currently in the process of writing the first of many books she has plans to write, all of which will be designed to help readers live their best life.

Learn more at www.lovesmosaic.com

JENNIFER SMITH

Jennifer F. Smith is a mother, a therapist, an author, and a mentor. She is a Chicago native and the founder of Black Butterfly Chicago, an organization that provides mentoring, advocacy, workshops, and mental health-based services to the community. She is the author of *Minesa's Mindful Day* and *The Feel of Color*, where awareness and creative storytelling collide to break the stigma around mental health. Jennifer is a licensed clinical psychotherapist who does public speaking and provides consultation and counseling services around Chicago. She enjoys helping others overcome adversities and transform trauma into stories of growth, empowerment, and resiliency. Jennifer has been featured at the Soulful Chicago Bookfair, is a monthly blogger for Begin Within Counseling and Coaching Services, Inc., and has been a special guest for various media programs, such as radio Rejoice 102.3 WYCA, WLLF Radio Network, and the Nonprofit Optimist podcast. According to Jennifer, "We are not blessed with gifts to keep them for ourselves, but rather to utilize them in uplifting others and glorifying God."

Contact her at blackbutterflychicago@gmail.com

MARA MONIQUE

Mara Monique's humble beginning into serving teens and, eventually, women came naturally. After working with high school students for over fifteen years as a motivational mentor, encouraging students with personal and scholarly achievements, Mara Monique set out to create a carefree space where women can rejuvenate themselves. She established Rejoov Retreats Bed & Breakfast in Jamaica, where she works as the owner and operator. It is a place where women can focus on their wants and needs to purposely reboot their minds, bodies, and spirits. There, she promotes everyone's self-love and self-care as the way to regain balance and peace in their lives and provides a comfortable space where peace from life's stressors is easily found.

Mara Monique has a knack for assisting people to find the positive in any situation when given the opportunity. She lives by the saying, "where there's a will, there's a way." If you have the will, she'll help you find a way.

Learn more at www.rejoovretreats.com or
email at MaraMonique@rejoovretreats.com

TASHA CHAMPION

Tasha Champion is a certified master life coach who specializes in helping women in the areas of self-love, authentic happiness, purpose, and spiritual growth. After finding herself a divorced single mom of four who could not identify who she was in the mirror, Tasha started working with a life coach and began to spiritually search for answers. Through her own healing, she discovered purpose and launched Champion EmpowHERment. Her motto, "Love the Champion You Are," speaks to her belief that there is a Champion inside each of us. She encourages and guides women to own their power, beauty, and truth. She credits this belief and her unwavering faith as the spiritual medicine that got her through a breast cancer diagnosis, chemotherapy treatments, and multiple surgeries. She continues to use her experience to reach other women and empower them to Love the Champion they are.

Contact her at tasha@tashachampion.com

TIFFANY ADAMS

Tiffany Adams has been in the medical field for the last fifteen years. She enjoys helping people and is a dedicated and loving mother of two amazing girls. She credits God for all of her accomplishments in her life. Tiffany has dedicated her life to helping people of God and takes daily prayer requests for anyone who seeks prayers. She enjoys reading and taking her children on vacations; their favorite spot is Disneyland and they are eager to go again this year!

> If you would like to get in touch with Tiffany,
> she can be contacted through her email at
> tiffany.adams88@yahoo.com

YOLANDA ALLEN

Yolanda Allen is an educator, wife, and proud "Girls Mom" of three birth daughters and one bonus daughter. She credits developing a serious illness while visiting China as the catalyst that forever changed her views on parenting and partnering. Facing the possibility of not living to see her girls become women, she decided to L.O.L.: Live Out Loud.

Contact her directly at yawifecoach@gmail.com

PERSONAL TRANSFORMATION SERIES

Kiana Shaw invites teens to attend LeadHERship Academy for a Personal Transformation Series. For more information and to register, please visit:

www.KianaShaw.com

Personal Transformation Series with weekly lessons for teens covering **life, leadership and professional development skills.**
Use code "**Diary**" to get your discount.

*This offer is open to all purchasers of "A Mother's Diary: A Daughter's Handbook" by Kiana Shaw. Original proof of purchase is required. The offer is limited to the online classes only and your registration for it is based on availability of space and/or changes to the program schedule. This is a limited time offer, expiring January 1, 2020.

CREATING DISTINCTIVE BOOKS WITH INTENTIONAL RESULTS

We're a collaborative group of creative masterminds with a mission to produce high-quality books to position you for monumental success in the marketplace.

Our professional team of writers, editors, designers, and marketing strategists work closely together to ensure that every detail of your book is a clear representation of the message in your writing.

Want to know more?
Write to us at info@publishyourgift.com
or call (888) 949-6228

Discover great books, exclusive offers, and more at
www.PublishYourGift.com

Connect with us on social media

@publishyourgift

www.ingramcontent.com/pod-product-compliance
Lightning Source LLC
Chambersburg PA
CBHW071913110526
44591CB00011B/1665